Beautiful Words

A Celebration for Word Lovers

CIDER MILL PRESS

BOOK
PUBLISHERS

13-Digit ISBN: 978-1-95151-154-8
10-Digit ISBN: 1-95151-154-9

This book may be ordered by mail from the publisher. Please include $5.99 for postage and handling. Please support your local bookseller first!

Books published by Cider Mill Press Book Publishers are available at special discounts for bulk purchases in the United States by corporations, institutions, and other organizations. For more information, please contact the publisher.

Cider Mill Press Book Publishers
"Where good books are ready for press"
501 Nelson Place
Nashville, Tennessee 37214

cidermillpress.com

Typography: Crimson Pro, Gotham
All images used under official license from Shutterstock.com and Unsplash.com.

Printed in Malaysia

23 24 25 26 27 COS 5 4 3 2 1
First Edition

rain
see page 168

sax
see page 181

"I know nothing in the world
that has as much power as a word.
Sometimes I write one, and I look at it,
until it begins to shine."

—*Emily Dickinson*

"So difficult it is to show the various meanings and imperfections of words when we have nothing else but words to do it with."

—*John Locke*

enigma
see page 74

library
see page 120

"As we must account for every idle word, so must we account for every idle silence."

—Benjamin Franklin

"Good words are worth much, and cost little."

—*George Herbert*

skyscraper
see page 187

waterfall
see page 225

"Words have no power to
impress the mind without the exquisite
horror of their reality."

—*Edgar Allan Poe*

Aa

absence
Noun | AB – sense

The state of being away or not present, or a lack of something.

With no phone and no email in the hut, he felt a complete absence of the type of cares that would normally weigh him down.

adventure
Noun/Verb | Ad – VEN - churr

A risk or chance, with a high possibility of going new places, doing new things, and meeting new people, often under auspicious ircumstances; to take such a risk or chance.

"I'm tired of living day to day," she announced. "I want to have an adventure!"

afar
Adverb | Uh - FAR

To or from a large distance.

The clock tower is clanging from afar over the valley.

afternoon

Noun | AFF – ter – noon

The period of day between noon and evening. When afternoon ends and evening begins tends to be subjective, but usually coincides with the sun starting to go down.

"Why don't we go to the beach in the morning," she asked, "do brunch around 11 or 12, then start driving in the afternoon?"

airlift

Noun/Verb | AIR – lift

The act or process of delivering people or things from one place to another, often under dangerous or controversial conditions; to airlift something or someone.

Starting in late June 1948, British and American air force pilots airlifted coal, medicine, and food into a blockaded Berlin.

alight

Verb | Ah - LIGHT

To descend, come down, or land gently or lightly.

The dove alighted on the railing and regarded them without fear.

alluvial

Adjective | Ah – LUVE – ee – ul

Describing a mass of waterborne matter deposited by rivers on low-lying lands surrounding the water.

The children would gather pebbles from the alluvial deposits along the creek and use them in projects.

amber

Noun/Adjective | AM – burr

Ancient sap hardened into stone over time; the color of said stone, which can be described as mostly yellow and darkening to brown.

By studying insects fossilized in amber, scientists hope to learn more about how DNA can be preserved over time.

amble

Verb | AM – bul

To walk at an easy pace, conspicuously.

They ambled down Beale Street, soaking up the sounds of blues music coming from the music clubs.

amulet

Noun | AM – yoo - let

A gem or other object carried as a charm or ward against misfortune or evil, often worn around the neck.

They thought she was superstitious, but really she just liked how the amulet looked on her.

alpine
Adjective | AL – pine

Pertaining to the Alps, or to any high mountains.

ancestors

Noun | AN – sess – ters

Those from whom a person has descended.

Though she didn't know what village her ancestors had come from, she wanted to get a sense of their home country.

anchor

Noun/Verb | ANG – ker

An implement for keeping a ship in a particular spot by temporarily chaining or weighting it to the bed of a harbor or river; to attach something to a particular spot, or to cast anchor.

The yacht dropped anchor in Montego Bay, where the guests would be able to get some snorkeling in.

ancient

Adjective/Noun | AIN – chint

Very old or belonging to long-ago times, or of incredible age; one who is ancient.

Methuselah, a Great Basin bristlecone pine, is more than 4,835 years old—more ancient than the Old Kingdom of Ancient Egypt—whose exact coordinates the US government keeps secret.

anise

Noun | ANN – iss

An herbal plant of the carrot family, the aromatic seeds of which are used in making cordials or as a flavoring ingredient in recipes.

arch
Noun/Verb | ARCH

A concave construction of stones or other
materials, built or centering over an open space,
so as by mutual pressure to support each other
and sustain a weight; to bend into an arch.

antiquarian

Adjective | An – TI – kware – ee – an

Connected with the study of very old things.

After the tour, the artist began noticing many of the city's statues with an antiquarian pleasure.

archive

Noun/Verb | AR – kive

The place in which public records or historic documents are kept; to place in an archive.

The archives are only open with special permission, but they have original first editions of some of the most famous comic books ever made.

arpeggio

Noun | Ar – PEH – jee – oh

A chord of which the notes are played in rapid succession, often repeatedly.

The arpeggio, or "arp," as many keyboardists call it, is a key feature of composer Philip Glass's work.

arugula

Noun | Uh – RUE – guh – la

A popular garden and grocery-store leafy green with thick, feathery leaves and a peppery bite, often used in salads or cooked in hot dishes.

He couldn't wait to get back to the city and order the wood-fired arugula-and-garlic pizza from his favorite bistro.

ash

Noun | ASH

A genus (*Fraxinus*) of tree, known for its useful wood, native to North America, or the solid but light residue of something having fully burned.

His new ash baseball bat made a lovely crack *sound whenever he got a good hit.*

astral

Adjective | AS – tral

Of or belonging to the stars.

"On an astral scale," the professor said, "the distance between Earth and Jupiter is like walking from your front door to the curb in front of your house."

atlas
Noun | AT – las

A collection of maps.

astrolabe
Noun | AS – tro – labe

An ancient instrument for measuring the altitudes of the sun or stars, latitude, or planetary positions, usually made from brass.

The astrolabe exhibit looked like something out of a steampunk fantasy, but, as the description said, it was a very useful tool for over 1,000 years.

attune
Verb | Ah – TUNE

To make one sound agree with another, or to connect in a harmonious way.

She felt that she was already attuned to her horse's spirit during her first ride.

aura
Noun | AWR – ah

A supposed subtle emanation coming from anything, or an impression.

"You have a very I-don't-think-we're-in-Kansas-anymore kind of aura—are you lost?"

azure

Adjective | Az – YUR

Sky colored, a soft blue,
or referring to a cloudless
day's sky.

balustrade
Noun
BAL - oo - strahd

A railing, consisting of
balusters connected
by a rail, forming an
ornamental boundary
to a balcony.

Bb

bakery

Noun | BAY - kerr - ee

A place where bread's foundational ingredients—flour, water, yeast—are first made into dough then baked into bread, pitas, naan, doughnuts, cakes, and other foods.

If you want a fresh baguette or croissant, and when the line is shortest, you'd better get to the bakery—or boulangerie, as they say in Paris—before 9 a.m.

balmy

Adjective | BAWL - me

Fragrant, mild, and soothing.

Arriving in Florida again, the first thing that always struck him when he stepped outside the airport was the citrusy, balmy air.

baritone

Noun | BARE - i - tone

A deep male voice between bass and tenor, or a singer with such a voice.

In a deep baritone voice, the host announced that their table was ready.

bark
Noun/Verb | BARK

The covering or skin of the trunk and branches of a tree; the sharp, loud sound cried out by a dog or similar animal; a small ship.

You can identify a locust tree in winter by its bark, which has pronounced running ridges and valleys and is uniformly gray.

barrel
Noun | BARE – ul

A cylindrical wooden vessel made of curved slats, or staves, bound with hoops, or something long and hollow.

The winery had made the old barrels part of the experience by turning them into high-top tables.

bass
Adjective/Noun | BASE

Low or deep, especially in sound; the low or deep part in music.

When the bass kicked in, the dancers on the floor really started moving.

basalt
Noun | BAS – awlt

The most common kind of
igneous rock, formed by
fast-cooling lava that has
high concentrations of iron
and magnesium and which
is hard and dark, almost
black, in color.

bayou
Noun | BY - yoo

The name given to the marshy, usually heavily wooded offshoots of lakes and rivers, especially in North America, and especially in the Deep South.

bayberry

Noun | BAY - bare - ee

A rounded, dense shrub (*Myrica pensylvanica*) with leathery leaves and bluish-gray berries native to eastern North America.

The group of bayberry shrubs she'd planted in the corner of the yard sustained the cardinals all winter.

beach

Noun | BEECH

The shore of the sea or of a lake, often sandy and used for recreation.

The beach had a totally different feel in November: no scent of sunscreen, no music, or colorful umbrellas, and chilly, gray wind blowing the sand.

bedrock

Noun | BED – rok

A layer of solid rock lying beneath the soil or sand.

Where the highway cut through the mountain, the exposed bedrock was white with icicles well into spring.

behold

Verb | Be – HOLD

To look at with attention.

"Imagine yourself in your favorite place," she said, "then open your eyes: what do you behold?"

being

Noun/Verb | BE – ing

Existence, essence, or any person or thing existing; to have existence.

Gazing up at the point of light the astronomy app had identified as Mars, he wondered if human beings would ever land there.

billow

Noun/Verb | BIL – oh

A large wave swelled by the wind; to roll or flow in large waves.

The cat jumped under the sheet when she made it billow.

bioluminescent
Adjective
BY – oh – loom – eh – NESS - ent

Capable of giving off a type of light
which is produced by living organisms
through internal chemical reactions.

birch

Noun | BIRCH

Several species of trees belonging to the *Betula* genus, having papery bark and some, like the white birch, having smooth, white bark, prized for their graceful, slender appearances, thin leaves, and colorful trunks and branches.

One of the most popular trees distributed by the urban reforestation program is the river birch, because it is a native species, grows fast, and looks beautiful in the yard.

birth

Noun/Verb | BERTH

The act of bearing or bringing forth new life or something new, or the origin of something; to give birth.

The zoo's social media accounts proudly announced the birth of the baby hippo.

bog

Noun | BOG

Soft, mushy ground having a unique ecosystem, noticeably populated by mosses.

Through the bog, the catwalk carried the trail, but there was a mud smear where someone had obviously slipped and fallen in, then climbed back out.

book

Noun/Verb | BOOK

An assemblage of pages, usually of paper, bound inside a cover; to make a reservation.

They say his suitcase was always half-full of books, half of clothes, even when he traveled to Africa on safari.

booth

Noun | BOOTH

A hut or temporary structure made with light materials, a covered stall at a fair or market, or, in a restaurant, a large table with upholstered benches.

"Whenever I go into a crowded restaurant and see a cozy booth empty and available," he told his date, "a happy feeling comes over me."

botanical

Adjective | Bo – TAN – i – kul

Of or relating to the study of plants.

Her interests in any book were largely botanical, which was no surprise: she was a botany graduate student.

bothy

Noun | BAHTH – ee

A humble cottage or hut, especially when used as temporary housing for people engaged in hard manual labor in parts of Scotland.

They made haste for the bothy that overlooked the loch, which would at least get them out of the rain for the night.

boulder

Noun | BOWL - der

A large stone, usually too large for an adult to pick up, and sometimes massive, the size of a house or even larger.

While the playground was nice and the skating rink full of excitement, the kids' favorite part of Central Park was the giant schist boulders rising out of the ground.

briar

Noun | BRY – er

A prickly shrub, or the thorn of such a shrub.

He found the baseball but got caught in the briars and had to free himself slowly.

breakfast

Noun/Verb | BREK – fust

The first meal of the day, representing the breaking of the overnight fast; to have breakfast.

The hostel served a breakfast of Weetabix and hard-boiled eggs, along with instant coffee, in the common room.

bunch

Noun/Verb | BUNCH

A number of things tied together or growing together, or something appearing in the form of a tuft or knot; to swell out in a bunch.

Taco night was the day after tomorrow, so she grabbed a bunch of cilantro while she was at the supermarket.

bunny

Noun | BUN – nee

A diminutive or cute name for a rabbit.

In May, there was a new baby bunny living in the yard that liked to nibble on the herbs in the kitchen garden, which nobody minded because it was so cute.

buoyant

Adjective | BOY – yunt

Borne up above water or air due to being lighter, or vivacious and cheerful.

After the team's away victory, against their fiercest rivals, the whole town was buoyant the next day.

burst

Verb/Noun | BIRST

To break apart or break open suddenly, or to break into a sudden expression of feeling; a sudden outbreak.

With a burst of speed, the striker took the ball past the goalkeeper and scored.

butte

Noun | BYOOT

An isolated hill standing distinct from its surrounding flatter terrain.

The coyotes are known to gather and howl on the top of the butte.

butternut

Noun | BUTT – er – nut

The white walnut tree (*Juglans cinerea*), native to eastern North America, or a type of squash known for its use in pies and soups.

He carved his first candlestick from butternut, because he'd heard it was one of the easiest woods to work with.

buttress

Noun/Verb | BUTT – ress

A support pillar built onto the outside of a wall, especially in the case of Gothic cathedrals, or any prop; to prop up, as by a buttress.

She used data from several scientific studies to buttress her argument.

Cc

cadence

Noun | KAY - dense

The beat and rhythm of language or some other regularly recurring thing.

Despite her long practice using the language app, getting used to the cadence of the Spanish language was taking more time than she had thought it would.

caboose

Noun | Kuh - BOOCE

The last car in a train, usually intended for the use of the train's crew, or a slang term for buttocks.

The caboose had its heyday during the whistle-stop political tours in the early 20th century, when candidates would stand at the railing and give their stump speeches before the train steamed on.

cairn

Noun | KAIRN

A pile of stones used as a landmark on a mountaintop, especially to mark a trail where vegetation is minimal.

In the snow, it would have been impossible to follow the trail to the hut if it weren't for the cairns.

cake

Noun | KAKE

A pastry made out of sweetened, baked dough that is then formed into a flat or layered shape, round or otherwise, and decorated with icing, fruits, frosting, or other sweet ingredients.

calligraphy
Noun | Ka – LIG – ra – fee

A charactersitic style of writing marked by sweeping, graceful, continuous strokes made with fountain pens or specialized art markers, often used in invitations to formal events or in other cases where a script display type is called for.

In the Arab world, the writing is already calligraphy, and a lot of Arabic art is based on the display of script.

calm
Adjective/Noun/Verb | CALM

Still, quiet, serene, or absent of wind; serenity of feelings or actions; to make calm or to quiet.

Outside, after the loud metal concert, the streets were calm by comparison.

canvas
Noun | CAN – vas

A coarse cloth made of hemp, formerly heavily used for sails, tents, etc., and for painting on.

Using watercolors on paper is nice, but she prefers the tactile sensation of painting with oil on canvas.

campanile

Noun | Kam – pa – NEEL

A tower built to house
one or more bells.

carafe
Noun | Ka – RAF

A water bottle for the table, usually made of glass.

The glasses clinked against the carafe of water as the server approached their table.

carriage
Noun | KARE – ij

The act of carrying, or, in the preautomobile era, a steam or horse-drawn vehicle for carrying, or behavior or bearing.

The baron's carriage, drawn by two dappled gray horses, rattled up the cobbled incline to the palace on the hill.

cascade
Verb | KASS - kade

To fall gently by gravity, usually over a series of rocky outcroppings, or, as in the case of long hair, in waves.

The mountain stream cascaded over the lip of a large, flat rock and splashed into a clear pool below.

cask
Noun | KASK

A small, barrel-like, hollow round vessel for holding liquor.

When the pirate ship sank, the spot where it went down was marked by loose timbers and floating rum casks.

celestial

Adjective | Seh – LESS – ti – ul

Heavenly, or dwelling in the sky, stars, or heavens.

cerulean

Adjective | Seh – RU – lee – an

Having the deep deep, rich blue of a cloudless sky.

cathedral

Noun | Ka – THEE – drull

A large and lavishly built church, often of stone, very old, and with Romanesque or Gothic design features.

The cathedral of St. Barbara in Kutná Hora, with its three high, narrow spires and its bulky flying buttresses, is an impressive sight.

centrifugal

Adjective | SEN – tri – fyoo – gul

Relating to the force directed toward the center of a circle constantly required to keep a body moving in a curve instead of in its natural straight line.

The poi artist twirled ropes weighted with flaming weights, creating dazzling patterns with centrifugal force.

chalice

Noun | CHAL – iss

A cup or bowl, especially ornate or reserved for ceremonial purposes.

The chalice was passed down one side of the table and then the other, with each person taking a single sip from it.

chamois

Noun | SHAM - wah

A dexterous, hooved mountain animal, similar to a goat, that lives in the Alps and other mountain ranges in Europe, or a leather made from the skin of this animal.

You may need your binoculars to see the chamois, as they're quite timid, and distances in the High Tatras can be great.

cheer

Noun/Verb | CHEER

A happy frame of mind or joy, or a shout of approval or welcome; to comfort, encourage, or applaud.

The visit from her grandchildren and great-grandchildren filled her with cheer.

chiaroscuro

Noun | Key – AR – oh – skur – oh

In art, blending light and shade, or the art of representing light in shadow and shadow in light.

Eighteenth-century painters experimented heavily in chiaroscuro, using candles and twilight landscapes to achieve a range of dark and light values.

chickadee

Noun | CHIK – uh – dee

North American songbird of the genus *Poecile* known for its singing ability and dark crown contrasting with its white body, as with the universally recognized black-capped chickadee.

The chickadee is a great bird to get kids started on birding with, because of its unique appearance and its telltale song: chick-a-dee-dee-dee-dee.

chirring

Noun | CHIR – ing

The droning chirping sound made by crickets and grasshoppers.

While it was hot in the tent even at night, the chirring of the crickets made it easy to go to sleep.

chorus

Noun | KOR – us

A group of singers singing all at once; that which is sung by a chorus; the most emphatic and memorable part of a song.

As the singer reached the chorus of the song, everyone in the pub joined in.

cinema

Noun | SIN – eh – mah

The art of film/motion pictures, or the building where movies are shown.

Going to the local cinema on a rainy Sunday afternoon and seeing the latest indie comedy was one of her greatest pleasures.

clay

Noun | KLAY

Firm, moldable earth, at times dried into shapes such as bricks or pottery.

The soil was mostly clay, so every time it rained it tended to stay wet in the fields.

clink

Noun/Verb | KLINK

A ringing sound made by striking together sounding bodies, as in stone on stone or glass on glass; to make such a sound.

After the wedding toast was raised, the reception hall filled with the happy sound of many glasses clinking.

cloister

Noun/Verb | KLOY – stir

A place of religious seclusion with others, a monastery or convent, or an enclosed place; to confine in a cloister.

While the members of the cloister had unusual daily habits, they were well-known for their superior printing skills and vocal abilities.

cloth

Noun | KLOTH

Woven material from which clothing or other fabric items are made.

One part of the restaurant's effort to go green was to begin using cloth napkins instead of disposable paper ones.

cloud

Noun/Verb | KLOWD

A mass, consisting of minute particles of water, often in a frozen state, floating in the atmosphere; a multitude of anything; anything that obscures something else; to darken or become darkened.

A series of cumulus clouds hung still in the blue sky, showing that the day would be a calm one.

coast
Noun/Verb | KOAST

The edge of land next to the sea, often the
border of a country; to travel with little to
no effort, as in downhill on a bicycle.

clove

Noun | KLOVE

The unexpanded flower of the clove tree (*Syzygium aromaticum*), a native of the Moluccas, used as a spice, or the flavor of such.

It was September, so she stocked up on allspice and clove to make her own batch of pumpkin spice to add to her coffee.

comfrey

Noun | KOMM – free

Plants of the genus *Symphytum,* of the borage family, long used in herbal medicine and gardening.

He harvested several large leaves from the bushy comfrey plant to be used in his organic fertilizer tea.

communal

Adjective | Cah – MYOON – ul

Owned and shared collectively, or by the members of a commune.

The bikes in the courtyard were communal and free to use by any of the building's tenants.

complement
Noun/Verb | KOM – ple – ment

That which completes or fills a lack, or adds to the experience of something else; full number or amount; to complete or fill a lack.

A large cup of boardwalk fries, dowsed in vinegar, is the perfect complement to a day at the beach.

Conestoga
Noun | KON – eh – STOW – gah

A large horse-drawn wagon used to carry settler families west in the expansion of the early United States.

At night on the prairie, the men would keep the fire going all night long, in the middle of the circle formed by the Conestoga wagons.

contour
Noun/Verb | KON – toor

An outline, or the line which encapsulates the figure of any object; to mark with contour lines.

He could tell by the tight contour lines on the topographical map that the climb would be very steep.

convergence
Noun | Kon – VER – jence

The act or state of coming to one point.

The convergence of the Monongahela and Allegheny Rivers into the Ohio River has always made Pittsburgh a special place, geographically.

copse
Noun | KOPS

A grove of small trees or brushwood, sometimes used for periodic cutting.

When he heard from a villager that the war was over, the soldier buried his uniform in a nearby copse of trees and began his long journey home.

core
Noun | KOR

The central or inner part of anything, especially of fruit, the Earth, or the human body.

After the bicycle trek ended in hours of steady rain, it took him a long, hot shower and wearing cozy clothes by the fire until his core temperature came back up to normal.

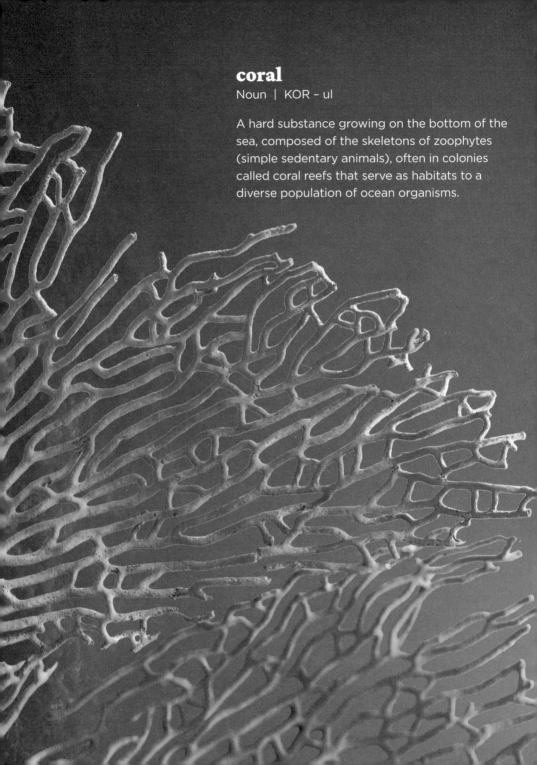

coral
Noun | KOR – ul

A hard substance growing on the bottom of the sea, composed of the skeletons of zoophytes (simple sedentary animals), often in colonies called coral reefs that serve as habitats to a diverse population of ocean organisms.

cornflower

Noun | KORN – flow – er

Centaurea cyanus, aka bachelor's button, a purplish-blue-flowering plant from Europe once seen as a weed in North American cornfields; a shade of blue.

Seeing the cornflowers bloom always made her feel like summer was really happening.

corvid

Adjective | KOR – vid

Pertaining to the crow (*Corvus* "genus").

He noticed the crow watching him, cocking its head with corvid intelligence, as he carried his one bag of trash to the curb.

cosmic

Adjective | KOZ – mik

Referring to the universe as a whole.

On a cosmic scale, even the Milky Way galaxy is just a drop in the ocean.

cotton

Noun | COT – en

A soft, white substance harvested from the pods of the cotton plant, a shrub belonging to the *Gossypium* genus; cloth made of cotton.

cradle

Noun/Verb | KRAY – dul

A crib in which children are rocked; infancy, or place where infancy occurs; to rock in a cradle, or to nurture.

In preparation for her own daughter's imminent arrival, she bought fresh bedding for the antique cradle.

crescent

Adjective/Noun | KRESS – ent

Shaped like a moon partially obscured or a new or old moon; anything having such a shape.

The sheet of crescent-shaped cookies was fresh out of the oven and ready to be sprinkled with powdered sugar.

crossroads

Noun | KROSS – rodes

The point where two roads meet, crossing each other.

The taco truck set up shop at the crossroads.

crystal

Noun | KRISS - tul

An assemblage of chemicals or chemical compounds into an aesthetically pleasing shape; such a compound tending to shimmer, letting through or reflecting light due to its flat, angular surfaces.

Looking through the clearest piece of quartz crystal she'd ever seen, she thought she could see the moon in a dozen different facets.

curtain

Noun/Verb | KUR – ten

Drapery cloth hung on the inside of a window to block the view, weather, or light, or, in theater, at the edge of a stage to conceal the performers and set; to enclose or furnish with curtains.

When the curtain went up, the audience was looking at a stage set like a Parisian streetscape in the mid-19th century, complete with gas lamps and soldiers.

cypress

Noun | SIGH – press

Any evergreen tree or shrub of the family Cupressaceae, with small overlapping leaves that resemble scales.

They plucked a few green twigs of cypress to take back home for a vibrant, pine-tasting tea.

Dd

daffodil

Noun | DAF – oh – dil

A perennial yellow spring flower (*Narcissus pseudonarcissus*) that grows from bulbs.

The daffodils, yellow and white, under the trees gave the orchard a fairy-tale look.

damask

Noun/Adjective | Da – MASK

Firm, decorative cloth woven through with patterns, often flowery; a reddish color.

The original damask wall covering, depicting a pastoral forest scene, was protected behind a fiberglass shield.

dance

Verb/Noun | DANTS

To move with measured steps to music; the movement of one or more persons to music.

Every Thursday night, the cantina came alive with the sound of salsa music and the sashaying of couples dancing the salsa.

dappled
Adjective | DAP – ulled

Marked with spots or blots.

The surface of the pond under the birch trees was dappled with midday sunlight.

dawn
Noun/Verb | DAWN

The time when night becomes day, or a beginning; to become day, to begin to grow light, or to begin to appear.

The fisherman and his son steered the boat out of the harbor at dawn, as the trees at the top of the hill were just turning orange.

daydream
Verb/Noun | DAY – dreem

To speculate or indulge one's fancies; a reverie or wishful thinking.

She often daydreamed about buying a coffee shop or bakery in a quaint village somewhere.

delta
Noun | DEL – ta

A triangle-shaped area of land formed at the mouth of a river.

The Mississippi Delta is a region unto itself, once the most fertile cotton-producing land in the world.

deciduous

Adjective | Dee – SID – yoo – us

Characterized by falling in autumn, as leaves, or denoting a tree whose leaves fall in autumn.

depth

Noun | DEPTH

The measure of deepness down or inward, or a deep place, the sea, or the middle.

What the music lacks in rhythm it makes up for in depth, with layers of instruments creating a complex soundscape.

diamond

Noun | DYE – mund

The most valuable of gems and the hardest of all substances, or, in geometry, a four-sided figure with two wide and two acute angles.

The diamond on her engagement ring was the most valuable thing she owned.

dim

Adjective/Verb | DIM

Obscured, as by low light or large lengths of time; to darken.

The swans glided silently across the dim lagoon.

dimension

Noun | Di – MEN – shun

Distance measured in length, width, or height, the combined measurements which constitute how much space an object takes up; a plane of existence or awareness.

She's been honing her craft for so long that when she sits down with her tools, she's working in a different dimension than the rest of us.

discover

Verb | Diss – CUV – er

To find, find out, or expose something formerly hidden, secret, unknown, or hard to reach.

The land they discovered was not the land they thought they were going to discover, but an entirely different one.

doorway

Noun | DOR – way

The entrance or passage closed by the door.

She gave me directions: we go down the long hall, turn left, through the open doorway, then second door on the right.

dove

Noun | DUV

A pigeon, such as a mourning
dove, or a person who advocates
for peace and de-escalation.

dory

Noun | DOR – ee

A small, strong, flat-bottomed rowboat with a sharp prow.

It had been many years since he had rowed the old wooden dory across the lake, but today was a special occasion.

dreams

Noun | DREEMS

A series of thoughts and imaginative flights of fancy during sleep, or visions of ideal futures.

The band was headed to Seattle with the windows down and dreams of selling out all three nights.

driftwood

Noun | DRIFT – wood

Wood drifted or floated by water.

The girl asked her mother if she could take the piece of smooth driftwood she found in the creek back home.

dune
Noun | DOON

A hill of sand on the seashore
or in the desert.

Druid

Noun | JRU – id

A priest or priestess among the ancient pagan Celts of Britain, France, and Germany, who worshipped under oak trees and in forest settings.

The Druids would begin ceremonies by drumming and chanting the praises of the spirits of the forest.

dulcimer

Noun | DUL – sim – er

A guitar-like musical instrument played by striking the strings with a small cork-headed hammer in each hand.

When she saw a man with a long gray beard tuning a dulcimer, she knew the show was going to feature some genuine Appalachian Mountain music.

dusk

Noun | DUSK

Twilight, or partial darkness, especially just before night.

Whenever supper ran until dusk, they'd look up and see the bats zipping through the air over their heads, chasing bugs.

Ee

eddy

Noun/Verb | ED – ee

A current of water or air swirling back against the main stream and causing a circular motion, or a whirlpool or whirlwind; to move like such a current.

For a while, he watched the eddies swirling behind the pillar of the bridge.

eldritch

Adjective | EL – dritch

Weird, eerie.

During the day, driving, there was nothing special about the railroad crossing, but on a moonlit night and on foot it took on an eldritch quality.

electric

Adjective | Ee – LECK – trick

Pertaining to or produced by electricity, or showing high energy or enthusiasm.

She found the singer of the band positively electric in his movement around the stage.

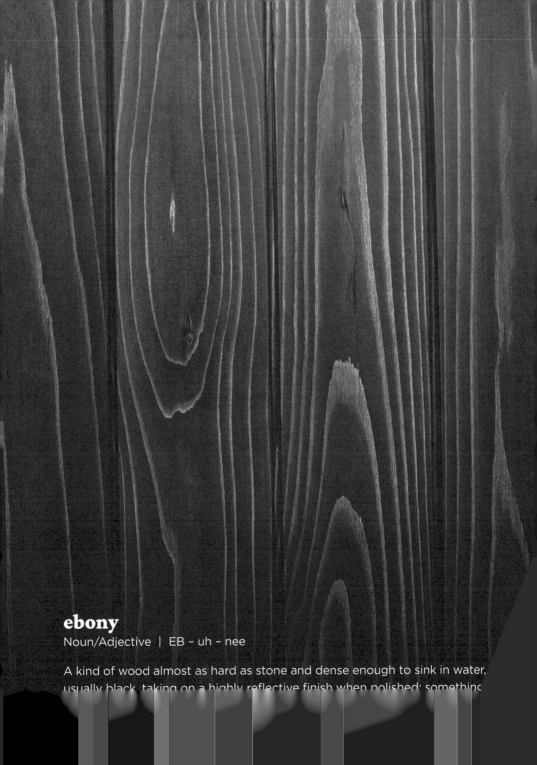

ebony
Noun/Adjective | EB – uh – nee

A kind of wood almost as hard as stone and dense enough to sink in water, usually black, taking on a highly reflective finish when polished; something

elevation

Noun | EL – eh – VAY – shun

The act of raising, or the state of being raised, or exaltation or happiness, or an elevated station, or the height of something in relation to a base point.

"At that high of an elevation," he explained, "you should take a few days to let your body acclimatize before doing anything strenuous."

elixir

Noun | Ee – LIKS – er

The quintessence of anything, a substance that invigorates, or a compound tincture.

His grandmother always called her apple mint tea the "elixir of summer."

elsewhere

Adverb | ELSS – ware

In or to another place.

He thought they'd gone upstairs to brush their teeth, but they must have gone elsewhere.

embark

Verb | Em – BARK

To go on board ship, or to engage in or begin any undertaking or journey.

Before embarking on their summer vacation, they made sure to check the air in the tires and to leave the spare house keys under the plant pot.

embrace

Verb/Noun | Em – BRACE

To take in the arms and press against the chest with affection, or to accept eagerly or willingly; an embracing.

They embraced, knowing it would be three months until they saw each other again.

emerald

Noun/Adjective | EM – er – ald

A much-prized mineral having a velvety green color; the color of an emerald.

She had a tumbled emerald at the end of her necklace: her birthstone.

enigma

Noun | En – IG – ma

Anything obscure or having a hidden meaning; a riddle or puzzle.

Every painting he showed felt like an enigma, which is partly why she enjoyed his work.

eschew

Verb | Ess – CHOO

To shun, abstain from, or keep away from.

He was normally one to scoff at the chance of danger, but even he eschewed the part of the river called "Dead Man's Drop."

estuary

Noun | ESS – tyoo – air – ee

The wide lower part of a river where it enters the ocean.

The estuary of the Amazon is over 200 miles wide.

everything

Noun | EV – ree – thing

All things, or all.

"Sometimes everything feels like it's happened before, right?"

expanse
Noun | Ex – SPANSS

A wide extent of space, or a vast area.

fall

Noun/Verb | FAWL

The season between summer and winter;
to drop down or descend.

Ff

familiar
Adjective/Noun | Fa – MILL – yer

Known, well-known, understood, recognized, or easy; a being, like a bat, cat, or rat, accompanying a witch.

Something about the scene in the movie seemed familiar… and then she realized that it was taking place in a coffee shop she once went to almost every week.

fantasy
Noun/Adjective | FAN – tuh – see

A mental image or extended imaginative caprice; a narrative genre involving the use of outlandish settings and strange creatures and races.

She read widely, but any classic book with swords, dragons, and magic—high fantasy—was her favorite.

far
Adjective/Adverb | FAR

Remote or distant, in terms of space and time or purpose; very much.

"Have you ever seen how far you can go on your local city bus?" the article asked.

fennel
Noun | FEN – ul

A widely cultivated herb whose stalks, leaves, and seeds are aromatic and used in cooking.

The best part of fennel, according to the chef, is the broad, white base—perfect for slicing into wedges or strips and throwing in a roast to give it a faintly licorice flavor.

ferry
Noun | FAIR – ee

A ship that conveys people and cars from one side of a river or bay to the other, usually making regular round trips.

"We need to catch the 9 o'clock ferry if we want to make it to Montevideo by lunchtime."

filigree
Noun/Adjective | FIL – i – gree

A kind of ornamental metallic lacework of gold and silver, formed into intricate patterns; something like filigree.

She caught everyone's attention with her silver-and-bronze filigree earrings.

fireplace

Noun | FY – er – place

The area constructed indoors, often of stone, brick, or slate and having a chimney conveying smoke and excess heat swiftly outdoors, where a fire can be kindled and enjoyed.

fizz

Verb/Noun | FIZ

To make a hissing or sputtering sound from bubbles in a liquid; frothiness or bubbliness in a drink.

Not knowing that her toddler daughter had earlier shaken the can of seltzer water vigorously, she shouted in surprise when the fizz spilled all over the table and onto her phone.

flannel

Noun | FLAN - ul

Soft woolen or other cloth of loose texture, typically in a regular, square pattern, or the garment itself, most often pajamas or a rugged long-sleeved shirt.

When he opened the box in the attic, he was suprised to find it full of his father's well-worn flannel shirts from the 1950s.

flaxen

Adjective | FLAX – in

Made of or resembling flax (*Linum usitatissimum*), the fibers of which are woven into linen cloth; blond, long, and flowing.

The flaxen-haired snowboarder, with her California surfer looks and personal style, became an icon of the Winter Olympics.

fleck

Noun/Verb | FLEK

A spot or little bit of something; to make such a spot.

Jackson Pollock is renowned for his abstract painting style of dripping and flecking different colors of paint over a canvas.

flicker

Verb/Noun | FLICK – er

To flutter with movement, or to burn or be lit unsteadily, as a candle flame; an act of flickering.

They closed the car door and looked up the hill: the flashlight coming down through the forest flickered in and out as the person carrying it passed through the trees.

flint

Noun/Adjective | FLINT

A hard mineral, a variety of quartz, from which fire is readily struck, or material used to make Stone Age tools; made of flint, hard.

The museum's video display showed how raw flint could be processed, with care, into a number of sharp tools.

forage

Noun/Verb | FOR – aj

Green fodder for horses and cattle; to go around and plunder food, often in the sense of wild foods found in nature.

She began a club in her city for people who liked to forage sorrel, wild garlic, and other urban edible plants.

forest

Noun | FOR – est

A large tract of land covered with trees and undergrowth, generally left to the wild.

Most of the action in the Grimms' fairy tales takes place in the forest, for good reason—forests were scary places in preindustrial Europe.

forge

Noun/Verb | FORJ

The workshop of someone who works in iron, using heat and hammers to shape it into tools and weapons; to shape by heating and hammering.

With steady, even strokes of the hammer, he forged the blade into a flat, regular shape.

flock

Noun/Verb | FLOK

A company of animals, such
as sheep or birds, who stick
together; to gather in a flock.

frond
Noun | FROND

The combination of stem
and leaf in certain plants,
primarily ferns or palms.

fortnight

Noun | FORT – nite

A period of two weeks' time, sometimes used ironically to suggest pretentiousness.

"If you're already planning to stay 13 days, you might as well add one day and make it a full fortnight, right?"

fountain

Noun | FOWN – ten

A spring or up-shooting jet of water, natural or artificial, or the source of anything.

The fountains sprayed out of the mouths of statues of various aquatic creatures—frog, fish, turtle, etc.—arrayed in a circle.

future

Noun/Adjective | FYOO – chur

Time still to come; about to be or what will be.

In the 1950s and 1960s, visions of the future were full of gleaming cities with flying cars and glass-domed houses.

Gg

gable
Noun | GAY - bul

On the exterior wall of a building, the triangular part between the tops of the walls on the sides and the roof.

The houses along the canals in Amsterdam have hooks extending from their gables, once used to haul heavy things to the upper floors.

gaiter
Noun | GAY - der

A covering of cloth for the ankle, fitting down upon the shoe, usually to keep the socks and interiors of shoes or boots free of dirt, dust, or mud.

She felt more confident taking to the trail in her gaiters—no more poison ivy on her ankles now.

gambol
Verb/Noun | Gam - BOL

To leap or move about in energetic joy; playfulness.

She loved watching the goats gambol in their pasture, jumping around and headbutting one another.

galleon
Noun | GAL – ee – yon

A large Spanish vessel with multiple decks
and high walls, used from the 16th through
18th centuries for carrying cargo and treasure
under armed protection.

Ganymede

Noun | GAN – eh – meed

The largest of Jupiter's moons, or in classical mythology, the youth who was a cupbearer to the gods on Olympus.

Scientists believe that, under its icy crust, Ganymede hides an ocean of water 60 miles thick.

garb

Noun/Verb | GARB

A way of dressing; to clothe.

They were the only ones on their flight to Dallas decked out in full cowboy garb.

gargoyle

Noun | GAR – goil

A projecting spout channeling the water from the roof gutters of buildings, typically Gothic cathedrals, often representing grotesque figures whose mouths serve as the end points of the spouts.

She ducked into a doorway to get out of the rain and, hearing a spatter, looked up to see a hideous gargoyle spraying water downward from its wide mouth.

gate

Noun/Verb | GATE

A passage into a city, enclosed space,
or any large building, or an entrance;
to supply with a gate.

garret

Noun | GARE – ett

The top room of a house, just under the roof, once associated with poets' or painters' affordable but spare lifestyles , or an attic.

Forget about trying to make a lot of money and then becoming a writer, the visiting author insisted; as Thoreau said, if you want to write, it's best to go "up garret at once!"

gastropub

Noun | GAS – tro – pub

A tavern, bar, or pub serving elevated cuisine.

They held hands as they walked to the new gastropub with the Korean barbecue menu they'd heard so much about.

gather

Verb | GA – thur

To collect, bring together, or assemble, as in to assemble a group of people in one place.

The best thing about fall in the backyard is gathering with friends for dinner parties under the garden lights.

gaucho
Noun | GOW – cho

A native of Latin America noted for virtuoso horsemanship, or a Latin American cowboy.

The gaucho and his friends went out before the storm to round up the startled cattle.

genre
Noun | ZHAN – re

A kind or style.

"If you want to succeed as an artist," the professor told the class, "pick a genre and play by its rules, but also don't be afraid to break them."

gild
Verb | GILD

To overlay or decorate with gold or a gold-like substance.

The hard case of the book, almost 200 years old, had been gilded on the front cover in the design of an apple tree.

glass
Noun/Adjective | GLASS

The rigid, translucent or transparent substance resulting from
silicone-based mixtures melted and then cooled into hardness,
used for windows, or a glass drinkware, or the amount of liquid
a glass holds; made of glass.

gingerly
Adverb | JIN – jer – lee

Softly, delicately, or cautiously.

She dealt with the subject of moving in together gingerly, given his reluctance to give up his home gym equipment.

glacier
Noun | GLAY – sher

A very slowly moving river or mass of ice, especially as found at the North and South Poles.

From the vantage point of the kayak, the glacier's edge radiated cold and appeared incredibly blue.

glissando
Noun | Gliss – ON – doe

In music, sliding up or down a scale.

At the park, there was a public piano, and before anyone noticed she had left their side, she was playing a twinkly glissando.

gloaming

Noun | GLOW – ming

Dusk, or twilight.

She was used to sitting out with her tea in the gloaming, watching the fireflies begin their nightly illuminated dance.

glow

Verb/Noun | GLO

To shine with warmth, or to be flushed in the heat of passion; shining heat or brightness.

He became a blacksmith because he'd always been fascinated by the way heat can make solid metal glow.

gondola

Noun | GON – doe – la

A long, narrow boat (typically 30 feet long by 4 feet wide) used as transportation on the canals of Venice.

She thought, You only live once, and paid the hefty fee for a private nighttime gondola ride toward the Rialto.

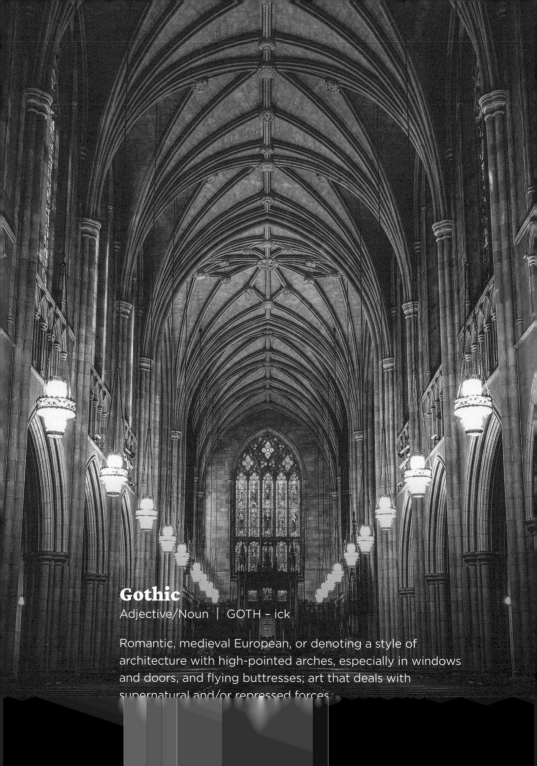

Gothic

Adjective/Noun │ GOTH – ick

Romantic, medieval European, or denoting a style of architecture with high-pointed arches, especially in windows and doors, and flying buttresses; art that deals with supernatural and/or repressed forces

gouache
Noun | GWASH

A method of watercolor painting with opaque colors, mixed with water and thickening agents, or work painted with this method.

good
Adjective | GOOD

Having qualities, whether physical, moral, or otherwise, that are desirable or suitable; something that promotes success; proper; effective; a lot; benevolent; that which promotes success, especially as opposed to evil.

It's a good thing you called me, because I was about to go by myself.

grove
Noun | GROVE

A number of trees growing together and taking on a pleasant, decorative character.

A grove of young walnut trees marked where the college botany program was conducting its study.

gulch
Noun | GULCH

A steep, narrow valley, ravine, or gully.

The herd of deer picked its way down into the gulch to look for water.

Hh

halo
Noun | HAY – low

A bright, sometimes shining ring around the head of a figure, often denoting holiness or angelic status, in a painting or in a figurative sense; a bright ring around the moon caused by light passing through ice crystals in the air.

The halo has appeared in art around the Buddha's head, as well as around the heads of Christian saints.

hamlet
Noun | HAM – let

A cluster of houses in the country, smaller than a village.

The hamlet's post office was still in operation, though only for four hours a day.

hammock
Noun | HAM – uk

A piece of strong, flexible cloth or netting suspended by the corners or the ends, often hung between two trees, and used as a napping spot.

From her position in the hammock, she could see the great, dormant volcano rising into the clouds.

happy

Adjective | HAP – ee

Having or enjoying pleasure or a sense of well-being, joy, or contentment.

When the letter turned out to be an acceptance, she was not only happy, she was ecstatic.

harbor

Noun/Verb | HAR – burr

A port for ships, or any refuge or shelter; to protect, to keep, or to take shelter.

Even at his age, he harbored dreams of summiting Mount Kilimanjaro.

harmony

Noun | HAR – mun – ee

A fitting together of parts so as to form a connected whole, or, in music, a simultaneous combination of sounds in agreement.

They had been jamming for almost an hour when they finally found their harmony, and what they were playing sounded, he thought, good.

harvest

Verb/Noun | HAR - vest

To gather the finished crops—vegetable,
grain, nut, or fruit—from the garden,
orchard, or field when ripe; the time or
result of such gathering.

haven

Noun/Verb | HAY – vin

An inlet of the sea or calm area of a river where boats can anchor, or any place of safety; to shelter.

Since there's a market, and a pub, and plenty of mooring space, this area of the river is a haven for longboats and their social interaction–craving drivers.

hazel

Noun/Adjective | HAY – zul

A shrub or small tree of the genus *Corylus*, yielding a nut enclosed in a leafy involucre; of a light-brown color, like a hazelnut.

Her eyes were green, her husband's blue, but both of their children were born with hazel eyes.

heaven

Noun | HEV – in

The sky; the dwelling place of God or the gods and the chosen blessed; a state of bliss.

She hadn't expected much, but the cheap bed-and-breakfast, with its view of the Tuscan coast, turned out to be heaven.

highlands

Noun | HYE – lunds

A mountainous area, especially in western Scotland.

The Highlands clans were famous for their bravery against the English occupation, their claymore swords, and their plaid tartans.

hike

Verb/Noun | HIKE

To walk a long distance, especially for recreation, sightseeing, or exercise, or a combination of the above; a long pleasant or strenuous walk.

Her dream was to hike the Pacific Crest Trail end to end, but she was starting to consider moving to Europe for a year instead.

hillock

Noun | HILL – uck

A small hill.

The farm was mostly flat, except for several wooded hillocks.

hither

Adverb/Adjective | HITH – er

To this place, or here; closer to the person speaking.

She did a double take because it looked like the drummer of the opening band was giving her a come-hither look from across the room.

holiday

Noun/Adjective | HAWL – i – day

A day off to be spent with family or friends, a consecrated or festival day, or a day set aside for the commemoration of a past event; cheerful.

As a child, her favorite holiday was Easter: colorful dresses, Easter egg hunts, and lots of sweets made it special.

hollow

Adjective/Noun/Verb | HAWL – oh

Not solid, or containing an empty space; a hole or depression in a body; to make an empty space in.

The hollow in the tree soon had new occupants: a pair of screech owls.

homecoming

Noun | HOAM – kum – ing

A return home, or the occasion when a group of individuals connected by a place returns to that place after an absence.

His homecoming from the war, in full uniform and wearing his medals, brought joy, pride, and relief to the small town.

home run

Noun | HOAM – run

In baseball, hitting such that the ball flies over the outfield wall and beyond the reach of the opposing team, enabling the batter and anyone else on base to circle the bases and cross home plate and score; a success on par with hitting a home run.

His home run in the eighth inning, which led to three runs scored, clinched the game for the Pirates.

honky-tonk

Noun/Adjective | HAWNG – kee – tonk

A rowdy dance hall or bar with dancing, usually playing country music, or the music itself, which frequently has lyrics describing vice and bad luck; something having those qualities.

She had had enough of fancy restaurants; she wanted to try a dive bar with a honky-tonk jukebox and a laid-back atmosphere.

hue
Noun | HYOO

Gradation in color, or
levels of color.

hub

Noun | HUB

The central node of a network, system, or structure.

The counter at Bell's Diner, known for its gossipy breakfasts and bottomless cups of coffee, served as the de facto information hub for the town.

hummingbird

Noun | HUM – ing – bird

Several hundred species of brightly colored, small, hovering birds, distributed throughout North and South America, that feed on nectar.

No sooner had she filled the feeder with nectar than three hummingbirds were buzzing around it.

Ii

ibex
Noun | EYE – bex

Wild goats of the genus *Capra*, living in mountainous regions of Europe and Asia.

Somehow, he realized, the ibex had climbed from the bottom of the ravine halfway up the nearly vertical mountainside.

ice
Noun/Verb | ICE

Frozen water; to freeze water.

She put the ice cubes in the pitcher and used a stir stick to swirl them around with the herbs.

igneous
Adjective | IG – nee – us

Produced by the action of fire, as in rocks formed from volcanic eruptions.

They learned about igneous rocks by handling obsidian, basalt, and granite.

inner

Adjective | IN – er

Farther in, or interior.

The point of meditating is to make it possible to listen to your inner being.

Inuit

Noun | IN – yoo – it

Indigenous peoples of the whole northern coast of North America, and spread over Alaska, the Canadian arctic, and Greenland.

The Inuit word for Greenland is Kalaallit Nunaat.

invite

Verb/Noun | In – VIGHT

To ask someone to join oneself to an event or place, or to summon or attract; such a summons.

She was happy to be invited to the wedding, but very nervous at being invited to speak.

iris

Noun | EYE – riss

The colored part of the eye.

He was fascinated by the new husky in the dog park; one of its irises was pale blue, and the other was dark brown.

island

Noun | EYE – lund

A landmass surrounded
on all sides by water; a
metaphorical lone outpost.

jacaranda
Noun | JAH – kah – ron – dah

A tropical tree (Jacaranda mimosifolia) growing in the Americas renowned for its showy, clustering purple flowers.

Jj

jamboree
Noun | Jam – buh – REE

A boisterous gathering, often large and with plenty of festivities.

The backyard barbecue grew to become such a jamboree that he started to worry about upsetting the neighbors.

jasmine
Noun | JAZZ – men

A large genus (Jasminum spp.) of plants hailing from the Eastern Hemisphere, typically shrubs or vines, of which many species have highly fragrant flowers that are used in cuisines and scented products.

While getting dressed for the annual New Year's Eve party, she added jasmine essential oil to the diffuser, filling the room with a sweet, exciting aroma.

jetsam
Noun | JET – sum

Objects intentionally tossed overboard from a waterborne vessel into the water, often to lighten the vessel's weight.

On the run from the Coast Guard, the embezzler left a jetsam trail of boxes of forged billing statements behind his speeding yacht.

jewel

Noun | JOO – uhl

A precious stone, usually worn as a decoration or treasured by its owner; a person or object that is highly valued.

Comedian Jerry Seinfeld owns a lot of rare and vintage sports cars, but the jewel of his collection is the 1955 Porsche 550 Spyder.

jocund

Adjective | JOK – und

Merry, cheerful, jovial, or having uplifted spirits.

She was glad Amy had been hired; her jocund personality made the weekly team meeting much more fun.

juniper

Noun | JOO – ni – per

A genus (Juniperus spp.) of aromatic evergreen shrubs and trees, the fragrant, spicy, berrylike cones of which are used in making gin and flavoring other ingestible goods.

As the park tour guide said, the juniper's berries, dark blue in appearance, are actually cones with especially thick, merged scales, and make for a pleasant, piney tea when they're dried out.

jungle
Noun | JUNG - uhl

Land that is heavily forested and wild, often associated with tropical climates and containing exceptionally diverse flora and fauna; a wild place

kelp
Noun | KELP

Algae seaweeds, known for their nutritional value and
their importance as a habitat for marine animals, that
grow to heights of up to 175 feet in cool saltwater
shoreline areas, often making up underwater forests.

Kk

karma
Noun | KAR – mah

The theory, based on Hindu and Buddhist belief, that one's actions have inevitable consequences and determine one's next life.

Posting the picture of the car keys he'd found felt like the good-karma thing to do—he hoped someone else would do the same if he ever lost his keys.

keep
Verb/Noun | KEEP

To retain possession of, hold, or maintain, or to remain; the innermost, strongest part of a castle.

The women and children of the tribe would keep watch over the corn, shouting to warn away the crows.

kerning
Verb/Noun | KERN – ing

In typography, adjusting the space between characters, the W and the A, for example, to improve readability and appearance; said space.

He had been working nonstop on the logo for hours, but it finally clicked together when he kerned the "E" and the "L" farther apart.

kettle

Noun | KETT - ul

A container or vessel, usually made of metal, used for boiling liquids.

It being a London office, with many tea drinkers, the electric kettle was kept in frequent use.

knight

Noun/Verb | NITE

In feudal times, someone of noble birth and well trained to fight, achieving a high military rank denoted by "Sir"; to create a knight.

The most notorious of King Arthur's Knights of the Round Table is Sir Lancelot, but the purest is Sir Galahad.

knot

Noun /Verb | NOT

A gathering of threads or the like entangled, or an intentional interlacing of parts of a cord by twisting the ends about each other and then tightening; anything like a knot; a nautical mile; to tie in a knot or unite closely.

The boy hopped onto the pier and quickly tied a bowline knot to lash the boat to the cleat.

Ll

lanai

Noun | La – NYE

A porch covered by a roof, often in tropical or subtropical areas.

He didn't mind sleeping on the lanai, since it was enclosed by screens and it cooled down at night.

land

Noun/Verb | LAND

Soil, earth, or the solid part of the Earth's surface; a country, district, or real estate; to set on land or on shore, as in an aircraft arriving at its destination.

The farther west they drove, the land took on entirely different characteristics and shapes.

lantern

Noun | LAN - turn

A container holding a light source that lets the light through.

Each of the scouts was given a battery-powered lantern for getting around the campground at night.

lavender
Noun | LAV - in - der

An herb with purple flowers whose oil is widely admired for its scent.

lavish

Verb/Adjective | LA – vish

To spend extravagantly or wastefully; extravagant.

In contrast to her 30th birthday party, held at a lavish spa retreat in the Adirondacks, her 31st was held at a bowling alley.

lenticel

Noun | LINT – i – sel

A cellular apparatus that, on the exterior of a plant's stems, branches, or trunk, allows the plant to exchange gasses with the atmosphere.

Black cherry trees have noticeable white, horizontal lenticels breaking up their smooth black bark.

level

Noun/Adjective/Verb | LEV – ul

A perfectly horizontal line or surface; horizontal or even with anything else; to make horizontal or flat.

She used the leveling app on her phone to make sure the painting was hanging exactly level on the wall.

library

Noun | LI – brare – ree

The room, building, or network of buildings where books are kept in an ordered arrangement, often public.

If you can't find the book on the shelves of this library, you can request it through the interlibrary loan program and it'll come from somewhere else in the country.

lichen

Noun | LYE - ken

A rootless, plantlike life-form made up of a symbiosis between two kinds of organisms, fungi and algae, usually growing on rocks and trees in charismatic colors and shapes.

As the group hiked on, she had to stop and marvel at the boulder, the entire side of which was covered in little tubular lichens.

lighthouse

Noun | LIGHT – house

A tower built to use light to warn ships or boats nearing shore of the proximity of rocks and other dangers.

The fund paid for the lighthouse to be given a fresh coat of paint every three years to protect it against the salty sea air.

lightning
Noun | LIGHT – ning

An electric flash occurring in the atmosphere usually followed by thunder.

Long after the storm had passed over them, they watched the quiet lightning streak across the sky in the distance.

liminal
Adjective | LIM – in – ul

In, of, or describing an in-between or transitory state.

After she'd taken the buyout, she wanted to do some writing in the liminal time between her old job and finding a new job.

linen
Noun/Adjective | LIN – in

Cloth made of the fibers of flax plants, known for its breezy, soft qualities; the bedding, napkins, or clothing made of linen; of or relating to linen.

At our bed-and-breakfast, we were instructed to strip the beds and put the linen sheets in the hamper before checkout.

listen

Verb | LISS – en

To hear or attend to, or to follow advice.

At one point the poet looked up and was flattered to see the bar's patrons were carefully listening.

loam

Verb | LOME

A muddy, breathable soil made of a balance of clay, sand, and silt, ideal for growing plants.

If you want to grow a backyard garden in compacted clay soil, first turn it into loam by adding sand and compost so the roots can spread out and get water.

loblolly

Adjective | LOB – lawl – ee

A kind of pine tree (*Pinus taeda*) of the southeastern United States seaboard.

The loblollies and saw palmettos gave the sandy, dune-spotted plain a leafy, exotic look.

locomotive
Noun/Adjective | LOW – co – MOW – tiv

A machine, especially a train, that moves from place to place; capable of locomotion.

The locomotive landscape of the mid-19th century must have been very different to experience than the automobile landscape of today.

log
Noun | LOG

A thick and bulky piece of wood no longer part of a living tree.

Seeing that the party was far from breaking up, he added another pine log to the firepit.

logarithmic
Adjective | LOG – uh – rith – mik

Pertaining to, or consisting of, logarithms, of which one is the power to which another given number must be raised in order that it may equal the former number.

The pH scale is an example of a logarithmic scale—a pH of 5 is ten times more acidic than a pH of 6.

lull

Verb/Noun | LUL

To soothe or quiet, or to become calm; a time of calm.

She lulled her baby to sleep by gently singing and rocking her in her arms.

luminous

Adjective | LOOM – in – us

Shining or having a light-radiating quality.

A luminous globe hung above the patio, where the party gathered on the couches.

A cat of the genus *Lynx*, having high haunches, a short tail, a ruff under its chin, and ears topped with tufts of hair.

Mm

malachite

Noun | MAL – ah – kite

A copper carbonate mineral having a silky green appearance and typically seen in gem form.

The malachite statuette of a bear had a soft, swirling green look that made her want to pick it up.

Mancunian

Noun | Man – KYOON – ee – an

A person from Manchester, United Kingdom.

Even the Mancunian had to admit that Glasgow's industrial techno scene was impressive.

map

Noun/Verb | MAP

A two-dimensional visual representation of a physical area, such as a building, city, continent, or body of water; to create such a representation or describe clearly.

As a geography graduate student, the first thing he did whenever he traveled was to draw by hand a map of the area immediately surrounding his lodgings.

mango

Noun | MAYN – go

Stone fruit originating in Southeast/South Asia, produced by the *Mangifera indica* tree, and known for its bright, tropical flavor and soft, peach-like texture.

marine

Adjective | Ma – REEN

Of or belonging to the sea, near the sea, or representing the sea.

The marine ecosystem of the Great Lakes is far different than that of the waters around the Galápagos Islands.

marlin

Noun | MAR – lin

A large fish of the Istiophoridae family, which can reach lengths of over 15 feet and weigh more than 1,800 pounds, notable for its long, spikelike bill and named

The blue marlin grows from a little speck to being one of the biggest, fastest fish in the ocean, swimming across the world.

marshmallow

Noun | MARSH – mell – oh

A sugary, spongy, usually cylindrical white treat often roasted over an open fire, and often paired with chocolate and graham crackers to make s'mores.

There was every kind of marshmallow—vegan, gluten free, jumbo, pumpkin spice—but no one had brought roasting sticks, so all the kids scrambled to go find usable twigs.

Mars
Noun | MARZ

The fourth planet in Earth's solar
system; the Roman god of war.

meadow

Noun | MED – oh

A level area of land primarily occupied by grasses.

It would be a long time before the conservation project would be reforested, but as a meadow it would still be home to many kinds of wildlife.

meander

Noun/Verb | Me – AN – der

A winding course of movement; to flow or move in a winding course or flow around.

The river meandered through farmlands, under rural bridges, and finally into the city.

mellifluous

Adjective | MEL – i – FLU – us

Flowing smoothly, richly.

He lay back in the lounge chair and enjoyed the mellifluous gurgling of the pond fountain.

mensch

Noun | MENCH

A person held in high regard, as one having extraordinary integrity.

His professor considered Ralph Waldo Emerson "a real mensch" for bailing his friend Thoreau out of jail.

metaphor

Noun | MET – a – for

Figurative language involving the putting of one thing for another which it may only faintly resemble, often to draw attention to the thing being described.

"The river is a metaphor for time," the poet explained.

milkweed

Noun | MILK – weed

Fleshy, flowering perennials (genus *Asclepias*) known for attracting pollinators and for the milky sap they exude when damaged.

Stooping to look under the milkweed's broad, heavy leaves, she found a new green chrysalis.

mist

Noun | MIST

Water vapor visible in
the atmosphere, or rain
in very fine drops.

minaret

Noun | MIN – uh – rett

A narrow, pointed turret or tower in a mosque from which the calls to prayer are delivered.

During Ramadan, the streets of Sarajevo routinely echo with the calls to prayer being broadcast from speakers in the minarets.

mirth

Noun | MERTH

Merriness, laughter, or noisy happiness.

Even from down the road, he could tell by the light coming out of the windows and the intermittent loud laughter that the tavern was full of mirth.

mitzvah

Noun | MITTS – vuh

A good deed, or an act of courage or kindness.

"You coming here and cooking for us when my wife is sick is a real mitzvah."

modillion

Noun | Mo – DIL – yun

An ornamental bracket used in the cornices of some buildings, especially some ornate architectural styles.

Leaning out the window, she noticed that each building on the block had curvy modillions holding up its roofline.

moldboard

Noun | MOLD – bord

A curved, metal plate attached to the front of a plow, train, or bulldozer used to lift and divert the surface layer of earth.

With a pair of oxen and his new moldboard plow, he was determined to finally make a till field out of the rocky slope.

mood

Noun | MOOD

A state of being or disposition of mind, often temporary.

She found that being able to look at nature in its fullness had a positive effect on her mood.

moon
Noun | MOON

The satellite that revolves around the Earth monthly and reflects the sun's light at night, but also such a satellite so orbiting any planet.

They climbed out of the third-story window onto their roof to appreciate the rare red moon.

moraine
Noun | MOR – ayne

An easily distinguishable line of rocks and gravel along the edges of glaciers.

He walked back and forth to make sure, but it looked like the glacier was an inch or two farther from the moraine this year.

morel
Noun | MOR – ell

Any edible mushroom of the genus *Morchella*, having a honeycombed brown appearance and often prized as a delicacy and served fried.

Morel season at the farmers market is intense—most people try to get there as soon as it opens.

morning

Noun/Adjective | MOR – ning

The first part of the day; taking place in the early part of the day.

Her morning run took her past the Victorian observatory at the top of Patterson Park, where she would pause to rest and watch the sun rise over the city.

mosey

Verb | MOH – zee

To walk around leisurely or walk somewhere while taking one's time.

After work, the three of them moseyed over to their favorite restaurant to celebrate.

mother

Noun/Verb | MUTH – er

A female parent, or a woman in relation to her child, or something that has produced anything; acting the part of a mother.

The mother dolphin showed her two baby dolphins how to swim sideways.

moss

Noun | MOSS

Flowerless plants, of ancient
evolution, that break down
the substrate upon which
they grow and which tend
to blanket shady, moist,
forested areas.

mound

Noun/Verb | MOWND

A man-made hill or hillock, or something like such; to create a mound.

The prehistoric earthen mound had been built in the shape of a huge serpent, whose impressiveness was best seen from the observation tower.

movie

Noun | MOO – vee

A filmed series of images and sounds that tell a story.

Of her top five favorite movies, only one had been made after 1999.

mud

Noun | MUD

Dirt or earth that has gotten wet to some degree.

March in the Midwest is all mud, everywhere, it seems, she thought as she sloshed through the woods in her boots.

murky

Adjective | MIR – kee

Dark, gloomy, or obscure.

When the boy startled the catfish, it flashed away so quickly it left the pond murky with muck.

Muscovite

Noun | MUS – ko – vite

A person from Moscow.

Muscovites are very intense about their soccer: there are five Moscow clubs in the top division, and each has its share of ultras.

music

Noun | MYOO – zik

A connected series of pleasant sounds, or the art of combining sounds over time so as to please the ear.

"While I love Scandinavian metal music the most," she said, "K-pop comes in at a close second."

mushroom

Noun/Verb/Adjective | MUSH - room

A broad name for fungi, especially those that are edible; to grow or proliferate in the fashion of mushrooms; to look like a mushroom or mushrooms.

muslin

Noun | MUZZ – lin

A breathable, plain-woven cotton fabric used in bedding, curtains, and photography backdrops; named after Mosul in Iraq.

To create the effect of a desert behind the actors onstage, the set designers dyed muslin curtains orange and yellow and aimed warm lights at them.

mustard

Noun | MUSS - terd

A sharp-flavored yellow condiment made from ground seeds of mustard plants (genus *Brassica*), or the plants themselves, which have yellow flowers.

He liked shopping at the European market because the mustard aisle was twice as varied as that of his usual grocery store.

mystic

Adjective/Noun | MISS – tik

Sacredly obscure, involving a secret meaning only revealed to a spiritually enlightened mind, or belonging to mysticism; one who seeks elevated religious feeling.

Burning little bunches of sage in her backyard always made her feel a bit like a mystic.

Nn

namaste
Noun | Na – mas – TEY

A greeting of respect in India now used widely in the practice of yoga.

Once everyone had returned to easy pose after the meditation, the instructor folded her hands in front of her and said, "Namaste."

nave
Noun | NAVE

The central part of a church, not including outer aisles or wings.

The priest and his acolytes moved up through the nave to reach the altar.

nestling
Noun | NEST – ling

A young bird in the nest, newly hatched.

The robins had built their nest low enough so that, with a stepladder, the kids could observe the nestlings when the mother was away looking for food.

newspaper

Noun | NOOZ – pay – per

A paper usually printed daily but sometimes weekly or even less frequently, and formerly often twice per day, that conveys the events that have happened in the area and the world since the most recent edition of the paper.

Her father always took the Sunday newspaper out to the front porch and read it cover to cover, and then they would work on the crossword together.

night

Noun | NITE

The time from sunset to sunrise, when the sun is absent from the sky.

Like many writers, he found he did his best work at night.

oarlocks

Noun | OR – locks

A set of simple structures
on the sides of a rowboat
on or in which to rest the
oars when not in use.

Oo

oats

Noun | OTES

The seeds of a grassy plant (*Avena sativa*, though a few other species are cultivated in much lower numbers) which are much used as food, after processing, often in the form of dried, shelf-stable flakes.

"A parfait of oats, plain yogurt, chia seeds, bananas, and berries is one of the best breakfasts you can eat," the barista told her.

ocean

Noun | OH – shen

The vast expanse of salt water that covers most of Earth's surface, or any of its major delineations (Atlantic, Pacific, etc.), or any huge quantity.

An experienced sailor with a crew and a large boat can sail across the Atlantic Ocean in only a matter of weeks.

ochre

Noun/Adjective | OH – ker

A pale yellow clay used for coloring; the color of ochre.

Aboriginal Australians have used ochre in their art for millennia.

October

Noun | Ock - TOE – bur

The tenth month of the year, occurring during fall.

The best time to visit New England is in October, he always felt, when the leaves are changing and every small town starts to feel like the setting of a Stephen King novel.

omnibus

Adjective/Noun | AHM – nee – bus

Covering many or applying to many scenarios; a four-wheeled vehicle conveying a number of people from one place to another; bus.

The word "bus" comes from "omnibus," which, in times past, referred to a horse-drawn wagon that could fit a large number of people.

orbit

Noun/Verb | OR – bit

The path in which an object in space moves around another, larger, object, as with a planet around the sun; to follow such a path.

While the Lost Generation refers to American expatriate writers, Picasso and other visual artists were in the same orbit.

owl
Noun | OWL

A carnivorous bird that hunts for food at night, known
for its hooting, large eyes, and swiveling neck.

orchard

Noun | OR – cherd

A garden of fruit trees.

The orchard ran up the side of the hill, and before the tree line, there was a ten-foot fence for keeping the deer out.

outback

Noun | OUT – back

A rural and sparsely populated area, particular to Australia.

He didn't know how long they'd be in the outback, so he packed plenty of sunscreen.

Pp

parabola
Noun | Pa – RA – bowl – ah

A curve, nearly U-shaped, that is symmetrical, used in mathematics to describe certain phenomena.

The roller coaster went speeding down then grinding up in a shape close to a parabola.

pastel
Noun/Adjective | Pass – TEL

Chalk mixed with binding agents and colors for crayons and used in art, or a drawing made with such; made using pastels, or having a soft color.

After mastering watercolors, she moved on to pastels, smearing large sheets of paper with huge dobs of chalky color.

path
Noun | PATH

A way marked by the work of feet, or a track, or a course of action.

The possums followed a barely traceable path through an opening in the fence to reach their yard.

pawpaw

Noun | PAW – PAW

A tree (*Asimina triloba*) native to North America that sends up fast-growing trunks from a shallow root system; also the edible fruit of the tree, which has a custard-like consistency and texture and a faintly mango or banana flavor.

The pawpaws, over the course of two decades, spread throughout the woodlot and made the paths feel like tunnels, but when the fruit ripen in late summer, it's to die for.

pearl

Noun /Adjective | PER – ul

A much-admired shining white gem, made of an iridescent, layered substance, found in several kinds of shellfish; made of pearls.

The Japanese practice of diving for pearls, which requires its practitioners to hold their breath for almost two minutes per dive, is becoming a lost art.

pebble

Noun | PEB – ul

A small roundish stone.

He lost his footing and stepped off the path, sending pebbles rolling, which then sent a few larger stones tumbling, and after that he was more careful.

peony

Noun | PEE – oh – nee

A large showy flower of the
genus *Paeonia*, that is red or
white in color.

perambulate

Verb | Per – AM – byoo – late

To walk for the purpose of observing or surveying the boundaries of a space.

The rancher took the state representative out to perambulate a tight line around the property.

percolate

Verb | PER – ko – late

To cause a liquid, often by boiling, to strain through small openings, or to filter.

She didn't even wait until the coffee was finished percolating before she poured herself half a mug.

peregrine

Adjective | PEAR – i – grin

Wandering, or of a wandering nature.

The youths with the motorcycles and dusty jackets struck the diners as a peregrine pair.

perfume

Noun | Per – FYOOM

A sweet-smelling scent, especially sprayed from a bottle and applied to the neck, wrists, and other areas and worn out of the house to special events.

If the occasion called for her best black dress, she always said, then it also called for her best bottle of Chanel perfume.

pewter

Noun/Adjective | PEW – ter

An alloy chiefly made of tin, or utensils or cups made of such an alloy; a dull gray color.

With the ground muddy below and the sky a pewter gray, she felt it was a good day to book a flight to Mexico.

phantom

Noun | FAN – tom

A vision of something perhaps unreal, or an apparition.

He saw a phantom face in the window of the old brick factory, he told his friends.

pillow
Noun/Verb | PIL – oh

A cushion stuffed with soft cotton for
resting the head upon, or any cushion;
to lay or rest on for support.

picnic

Noun/Verb | PIK – nik

A meal packed at home and taken to eat outdoors, usually in a park or scenic setting reached by some amount of walking as an excursion meant to be enjoyed together; to picnic.

Her favorite scene in Little Women *is when the girls join their easygoing neighbor, Laurie, and his English friends for the picnic with croquet.*

piedmont

Noun | PEED – mont

The type of landscape found at the base of mountains; foothills.

The most famous piedmont region in the world is the one in northern Italy, at the base of the Alps.

pilgrim

Noun | PILL – grim

Someone who travels a great distance to visit a sacred place, or a wanderer.

Joining the flow of travelers to Galicia, they felt the power of the pilgrim experience increase the longer they followed the trail.

pine
Noun/Verb | PINE

A tree that has needle leaves that do not fall in winter, marked by a roughly conical structure, and which reproduces through the dropping of pinecones containing dozens of seeds; to wish for something you have never had, or which you had once but lost.

The pine grove had been planted in the 1970s to be harvested as Christmas trees, but now the trees were all over 80 feet tall.

pith
Noun | PITH

The marrow or soft, spongy substance in the center of the stems of some plants.

The beetle laid its eggs in the pith of the dried-out flower stalk.

placid
Adjective | PLASS – id

Gentle, calm, peaceful.

The lakes high in New Hampshire's White Mountains are so placid looking at them makes your stress melt away.

plaid
Noun/Adjective | PLAD

A loose outer garment of woolen cloth in a striped, multicolored pattern, worn by the Highlanders of Scotland; like a plaid in pattern and colors.

She enjoyed nothing more than getting into her comfy plaid pajamas and reading a book.

planet
Noun | PLAN – et

Any of the massive bodies in our solar system that orbit around the sun, or any such body so orbiting a sun.

Astronomers have discovered at least three planets orbiting Proxima Centauri, but it's Proxima b—Earth sized, and at a habitable distance from its sun—that really has them excited.

pleasure
Noun/Verb | PLEZH – ur

Agreeable emotions, or gratification of the senses or of the mind; to cause to experience pleasure.

The pleasure of recognition is seeing yourself or your experience represented in art.

plateau

Noun | Plah – TOE

A broad, flat space on an elevated position.

plumage

Noun | PLOO – maj

The feathers of a bird in their entirety.

The cardinal's bright red plumage makes it the most easy-to-spot bird in the backyard.

poet

Noun | POE – et

The author of and/or one skilled in making poems, typically credited with a gifted imagination and playfulness with words.

During the reading, the poet began moving about the stage, gesticulating and changing the tempo and volume of her voice like a musician playing an instrument.

pond

Noun/Verb | POND

A small, enclosed body of water; to collect in a pond.

The pond was so clear that she could see the pebbles on the bottom, even where it was eight feet deep.

porcelain

Noun/Adjective | PORSS – eh – lin

A white, thin earthenware, containing kaolin clay, often used in fine dinnerware or glassware; of the nature of porcelain.

The porcelain tea set had been imported from Meissen, Germany, in the 1920s.

porch

Noun | PORCH

An enclosure before the doorway to a building, covered by a roof that tends to be separate from the main building's roof.

Something about the house was still missing, and she figured it out when she tried to read a novel on the porch: it lacked a porch swing.

Portugal

Noun | POR - chu - gall

A small country on the western part of the Iberian Peninsula, with a long shoreline on the Atlantic Ocean; part of Europe.

They'd never even considered going to Portugal until they saw the video ad—by the airline—depicting villagers harvesting wine grapes.

post

Noun/Verb | POST

A piece of timber set in the ground, usually as a support to something else; a station; a system for sending and delivering mail; to attach on or to a post, or to a visible position in a public place.

The rough-hewn Osage-orange post must have been standing in the field for over a century.

powwow

Noun | POW – wow

A ceremonial gathering with a festival atmosphere convened by indigenous North Americans.

The biggest powwow—the Gathering of Nations—takes place every April in Albuquerque.

prairie

Noun | PRARE – ee

A vast, even state-spanning, meadow, level or rolling, without trees, and covered with tall coarse grass, used as a habitat by a large variety of flora and fauna specially evolved to live there.

Once upon a time, one-third of North America was prairie, where enormous herds of bison roamed and grazed freely.

presence
Noun | PREZ – ense

The state of being present or calm, nearness to greatness, or an apparition.

The great scientist's presence was still heavy in his childhood home, now preserved as a museum.

primordial
Adjective | Pri – MOR – dee – ul

Original or first, as in at the beginning of time itself.

Primordial Earth was a place full of warm, shallow water and lots of strange, simple creatures and plants.

public
Adjective/Noun | PUB – lick

Of or belonging to the people, shared by all, general, or common; the people.

The industrialist donated his vast land holdings to be turned into a public park.

prism

Noun | PRIZ – um

A solid, transparent stone having a geometrical shape and flat sides that can break rays of light into separate colors, or any such medium.

puddle

Noun | PUH – dul

A shallow accumulation of water in a depression in an otherwise dry surface, after a rain.

One of the best things about June is jumping around in the puddles after a summer downpour.

pylon

Noun | PIE – lon

A large monumental gateway to ancient Egyptian temples, or the towers that carry power lines across the land.

Up close, the rusted metal of the pylon towering near the railroad tracks was almost beautiful.

pumpkin
Noun | PUMM – kin

Vine-growning vegetable usually
orange in color with ribbed, tough
skin, rich in nutrients, and frequently
used in autumn pies.

Qq

quest

Noun/Verb | KWEST

The act of seeking something, often in a romantic sense; to go in search of.

His long quest to find the world's oldest shark yielded fruit in Iceland's cold waters.

quince

Noun | KWINSS

Pear-shaped, dimpled yellow fruit of the *Cydonia oblonga* tree, best eaten in jelly form.

After dinner and then tea, the waiter arrived with a quince-ginger tart, compliments of the chef.

quiver

Noun/Verb | KWIV – er

A case for arrows, usually worn across the back by way of a strap; to shake or tremble in fright.

Robin Hood pulled an arrow from his quiver as the Sheriff of Nottingham and his men rode closer to the forest.

quartz
Noun | KWORTS

A mineral made of silicon dioxide,
occurring in crystals and large, very
hard rocks, sometimes transparent and
sometimes milky white or rose tinted.

Rr

radiance

Noun | RAY – dee – ance

The quality of emitting rays of light or heat, or shining with light; splendor.

With a radiance that couldn't be denied, she entered the gallery directly after her speech to mingle with the fawning guests.

radish

Noun | RAD – ish

An annual garden vegetable of the Brassicaceae family whose root is crisp and sharply flavored and eaten raw.

He returned from the kiosk with a stein of lager and a plate of raw, sliced radishes piled high.

rain

Noun/Verb | RANE

Water falling from clouds in drops, or a fall of any substance through the atmosphere in the manner of rain; to fall from the sky.

Aside from the Englishman, who was used to walking in the rain, the hikers stayed in the shelter of the lean-to.

rainforest

Noun | RANE – for – est

A forest having a closed canopy and different vertical levels of varying flora and fauna, where heavy precipitation is the norm.

With its silent movement and climbing ability, the South American jaguar is well suited for the rainforest ecosystem.

ramble

Verb | RAM – bul

To walk without a particular destination in mind, as though to take in the sights of a rural countryside; in speech, to jump from topic to topic in a seemingly unfocused way.

England's long tradition of rambling through the meadows and mountains has led to the country enshrining "the right to roam," aka "ramblers' rights," into law.

range

Noun/Verb | RAYNJ

A stretch of mountains or hills, or an expanse of values; to move between two distant points.

The Appalachian mountain range is one of the oldest on the planet, over a billion years old, predating animal life itself.

raptor

Noun | RAP – ter

A bird of prey with a hooked beak and sharp talons, including eagles, hawks, and falcons, that lives by hunting other animals; small or medium carnivorous dinosaurs, quick footed, that hunted in packs.

The sight of a red-tailed hawk, the most common urban raptor in the eastern United States, swooping through a park never fails to thrill onlookers.

ray

Noun | RAY

A beam or line of light or heat; common popular name for such flat, cartilaginous fishes.

From the kayak, they watched the rays dart gracefully back and forth along the shore.

realm

Noun | RELM

A kingdom, country, or province.

Over the centuries, through marriage, alliance, and conquest, the Habsburg dynasty added realm after realm of Central Europe to the Holy Roman Empire.

redwood

Noun | RED - wood

An extremely tall conifer
tree (*Sequoia sempervirens*)
growing in California.

reef

Noun | REEF

A line of rocks or coral lying on
the ocean floor in shallow water.

refuge

Noun/Verb | REF - yooj

Something that affords shelter or protection; to take shelter.

They took refuge down the hill, where the lightning was unlikely to strike.

remembrance

Noun | Ree – MEM – brence

The occasion or act of remembering something in order to keep it in the memory.

In remembrance of his great-great-grandfather's arrival in the country by ship, he rented a boat and cruised in the harbor, thinking about what it must have been like.

rescue

Verb/Noun | RESS – cue

To free from danger or violence, or to liberate; the act of rescuing.

The concerned neighbor called her friend with a bucket truck to rescue the cat stranded high in the tree.

resonant

Adjective | REZ – oh – nant

Returning sound by reflection or by creating vibrations in other objects.

The swimmers' voices echoed off the especially resonant walls of the canyon.

reverie

Noun | REV – er – ee

A series of unconnected thoughts or impressions occurring during a repose; the condition of being lost in thought.

Taking the bus home from work, he was so lost in reverie that he missed his stop and wound up in a suburb.

ripple

Noun/Verb | RIP – ul

The light movement of small waves along the surface of water, often in curves; to cause a ripple.

The copperhead snake sent out little ripples as it swam through the cypress swamp.

rivulet

Noun | RIV – yoo – let

A small stream or brook.

The kids watched the rivulets of rainwater trailing down the windows all during recess period.

roan

Adjective | RONE

A reddish-brown color, with spots of gray and white.

Watching his daughter's riding lesson, he admired the roan horse's feisty spirit.

rock

Noun/Verb | ROK

A natural composite of sand, dirt, and/or clay that has hardened to stone; to move or sway back and forth, or to make excited, or to be good.

In single file, they scrambled up the rock using their hands and feet.

rogue

Noun | ROAG

A dishonest person, vagrant, or mischievous, playful person.

After the stunt with the tricycles, the fraternity was beginning to earn back its reputation as a rogues' den.

rosemary

Noun | ROZE – may – ree

A fragrant evergreen herb (*Salvia rosmarinus*), Mediterranean, whose leaves are used to flavor food.

She picked a handful of rosemary from the garden and plucked the leaves, dropping them onto the potatoes to be roasted.

rufous

Adjective | RU – fus

Brownish red.

The side of the barn had a rufous color from the years of sun exposure.

ruby
Noun/Adjective | ROO – bee

A transparent red gem; deep
red in color.

saguaro

Noun | Suh – GWAR – oh

A column-forming giant cactus (*Carnegiea gigantea)* that can reach a height of 50 feet, native to the American Southwest and Mexico.

Ss

sacred

Adjective | SAY – cred

In religious contexts, set apart, dedicated, made holy, or proceeding from God, and in secular contexts, entitled to respect or veneration.

The mound enclosure complexes of the Middle Woodland period North Americans were clearly sacred, though experts can only speculate as to why.

sail

Noun/Verb | SALE

A broad piece of cloth or canvas, spread to catch wind in order to propel a waterborne vessel; the act of moving a vessel over water by wind power, or to conduct a voyage by wind across the water.

The couple planned to kick off their retirement by sailing the Intracoastal Waterway from Miami to Boston.

sanctuary

Noun | SANK – choo – wair – ee

A sacred place, or place set aside for worship; the part of a church around the altar; a refuge.

The inlet was a sanctuary for manatees, as there were no boats allowed and the water was calm and warm.

sand

Noun/Verb | SAND

Fine particles of crushed or worn rocks, a major type of Earth's surface covering, especially on beaches or in deserts; to grind down with sandpaper.

Berlin was built on sand, so it was no surprise that plenty of it ended up on the hotel's floors.

sap

Noun/Verb | SAP

The vital juice of plants; to undermine or weaken.

Every January, they set the buckets on the spigots to collect the sap from the maple trees.

sassafras

Noun | SASS – uh – frass

A tree of the laurel family, common in North America, and also the bark of its root, which is a powerful stimulant and once widely used to make tea.

"The sassafras tree is easy to spot," she told her grandson: it's a skinny tree that has billowy leaves that look like green mittens.

sautéed
Verb | Saw – TAYED

Cooked quickly in a pan over heat, often in oil.

Often the first steps in making any kind of chili involve heating the oil and sautéing the onions.

sax
Noun | SAX

Short for saxophone, a brass wind instrument with finger-keys, often used in jazz music.

The sax solo was her favorite part of the song: pure 1980s hedonism.

saying
Noun/Verb | SAY – ing

A phrase held in common memory that is usually imbued with wisdom through its long use and canny applicability; the act of verbalizing information out loud, as the participial form of the verb "to say."

As the saying goes, "Many hands make light work."

scintillating
Adjective | SIN – tuh – lay – ting

Throwing out sparks or sparkling, or dazzling.

Passing, rebounding, pressing—he had a scintillating game on the court tonight.

seersucker
Noun | SERE - suk – er

A thin, usually linen, fabric with puffed stripes, typically worn formally in hot weather.

The old man remembered a time when the official business of the state was conducted in seersucker suits, in unair-conditioned rooms.

sesame
Noun | SESS - uh - me

An annual plant (*Sesamum indicum*) native to South Asia, grown for its edible seeds and oil used for cooking, prized for its nutty flavor.

The green beans, fresh from the garden, came garnished with toasted sesame seeds and served over rice.

shadow

Noun/Verb | SHAD – oh

Shade caused by an object blocking a source of light, or a faint
appearance; to shade or darken, or to accompany close by, like a shadow.

shimmer

Verb | SHI – mer

To reflect light waveringly or glisten.

shine
Verb | SHINE

To be bright, or to give off steady radiance; to cause to shine.

The full moon shined down on the snow-blanketed field, revealing the pack of wolves moving stealthily.

shore
Noun | SHOR

The coast or land adjacent to a body of water, such as a creek or ocean.

The shore was covered in driftwood and bladder wrack—typical for a New England coastline.

shuck
Verb | SHUK

To remove or strip off a shell or outer covering.

The children were told to take a break from playing and shuck the corn.

sidewinder
Noun | SIDE - wine - der

A small rattlesnake (*Crotalus cerastes*) in the desert Southwest that moves by propelling its body sideways into the bushes.

He stood safely back and watched the sidewinder twist its way across the path.

sienna

Adjective | See - EN – uh

Orange-red in color.

The sienna foothills radiated the heat of the day even as the air cooled.

sigh

Verb/Noun | SIGH

To exhale in a long, deep, and audible way, or to sound like sighing; a long, deep, and audible exhale.

The grandmother sighed when her granddaughter refused to eat the broccoli but wasted no time in devouring the French fries.

simpatico

Adjective | Sim - PA – ti – co

Having shared values or interests, or of the same mind or opinion or nature.

"I wanted to talk to you separately because I feel like we're simpatico on this," she said as the waiter brought their menus.

skein

Noun | SKANE

A knot or several knots of thread or yarn.

He packed his suitcase, figuring that a weekend at the cabin would help him unravel the skein of worries in his head.

skyscraper

Noun | SKY – scray – per

A building of immense height, first built in North America in the 1880s and now usually having more than at least ten floors.

While five of the ten tallest skyscrapers in the world are in China—and all those were built in just the last ten years—the tallest is still the Burj Khalifa in Dubai, which has 163 floors.

slope

Noun/Verb | SLOPE

Any incline down which a thing may slip, or a direction downward; to slant.

It wasn't a steep slope, but after a while their legs started to burn.

snow
Noun/Verb | SNO

The crystalline form into which the excess of vapor in the atmosphere is condensed when the temperature is below freezing; to fall in snow.

The first snow of the season is the most exciting time for young wolves in the wild—they play in it ecstatically.

snowflake
Noun | SNO - flake

A light, delicate flake of snow that falls with others to constitute a snowfall.

From the warmth of the tent and their sleeping bags, they watched the snowflakes increase in number and begin to accumulate on the ground.

snowy
Adjective | SNO – wee

Covered or blanketed in snow.

Tramping through the snowy woods after school made them feel like explorers.

spiral
Adjective/Noun | SPY – rul

Winding around an axis
continually away from a
point; a spiral line.

soothe

Verb | SOOTHE

To please with soft words, or to allay hurts either emotional or physical.

The coach attempted to soothe her team after the defeat by praising their competitiveness.

spindrift

Noun | SPIN – drift

The spray blown from the crests of waves.

Off the coast of Cape Cod, the harbor seals lifted their heads amid the spindrift kicked up by the high winds.

spore

Noun | SPOR

A reproductive body, sent out by plant or fungus, that can withstand harsh environments and reproduce even after long dormancy.

The little stems of the moss would soon be sending millions of spores into the air to be spread throughout the forest.

spring

Noun/Verb/Adjective | SPRING

The season between winter and summer, marked by heavy rain, new plant growth and flowers, and baby animals; a source of water rising from below the Earth's surface to the surface; to jump; occurring or appearing during spring.

Spring around the city is when the shorts and sidewalk tables come out and everybody acts a little bit happier.

spruce

Noun | SPROOSS

Any of a species of coniferous tree belonging to the genus *Picea*, growing wild in the colder, boreal regions of the Northern Hemisphere, and whose wood is often used in the making of musical instruments, paper, etc.

In southern Canada, the boreal spruce forests stretch on endlessly.

steamboat

Noun | STEEM – bote

A boat or ship propelled by a steam engine.

Samuel Langhorne Clemens piloted steamboats on the Mississippi from the late 1850s until the start of the Civil War.

stillness

Noun | STIL – ness

A state of being silent, motionless, and calm.

After the heavy rapids, the group stopped paddling, enjoying the stillness of the water.

stippled

Verb | STIPP – ulled

Engraved or dotted with small points, as in artwork.

Using the awl tool in his pocketknife, he stippled the handle of his walking stick to give it a better grip.

stone

Noun | STONE

A hard mass of mineral matter from the Earth's crust.

The white cliffs were the strangest color of stone he'd ever seen.

strait

Noun | STRAIT

A narrow pass in a mountain, or in the ocean between two landmasses, or difficulty or distress.

North America must have been populated, experts agree, by people migrating across a frozen Bering Strait.

sunflower

Noun | SUN – flow – er

A plant of the genus *Helianthus*, having a large flower consisting of petals, often bright yellow or otherwise warmly colored, radiating out from a large central disk, whose seeds are edible and produce an edible oil.

string

Noun/Verb | STRING

A cord of narrow diameter, often made of plant fibers wrapped around each other, used for tying; to provide something with strings, typically a stringed musical instrument.

With the new nickel strings, the guitar sounded extra twangy and bright.

summit

Noun/Verb | SUM – it

The highest point or degree, or the very top of something, as in a mountain; to reach the top.

If they started up the mountain before dawn, they calculated, they would reach the summit by lunch and have enough time to get back down before nightfall.

sunrise

Noun | SUN – rize

The first appearance of the sun above the eastern horizon, or the time of this rising.

"When was the last time you stayed out until sunrise?"

surf

Noun/Verb | SERF

The foam made by the waves crashing; the sport or activity in which a board is ridden on cresting waves.

sunset

Noun | SUN – set

The sun descending below the horizon in the west.

Every evening, the group of old friends gathered on the pier to watch the sunset.

supper

Noun | SUPP – er

The last meal of the day.

Having a hearty supper with the same group of friends and dormmates at 6 p.m. sharp every day lent a solid footing to an otherwise chaotic freshman first semester.

symphony

Noun | SIM – fone – ee

A harmonious coming together of sound produced by a large number and variety of instruments; something resembling a symphony.

Even in plain, boring parks in the middle of the suburbs, one can enjoy a symphony of birdsong.

Tt

tabernacle

Noun | TAB – er – nack – ul

A place of worship or sacred place, based on tents used as temples in ancient times.

The acoustics of the Mormon Tabernacle in Salt Lake City are so well considered in the design that you can hear every voice in the choir clearly no matter where you are sitting.

taiga

Noun | TIE – gah

A coniferous forest ecosystem, cold, having a permafrost surface, and located just below the Arctic tundra.

The biggest taiga in the world is in Russia, and that's where you'll find the largest land carnivore, the majestic Siberian tiger.

tandem

Adverb | TAN – duhm

Moving one close behind the other.

The mother boar and her squad of piglets walked in tandem through the forest.

tapestry

Noun | TAP – ess – tree

A textile, often intricately decorated, used for covering walls and for curtains, or something having the rich complexity of a tapestry.

The Renaissance tapestry depicted a hunting party in the woods near a castle.

tarry

Verb | TARE – ee

To linger or delay.

After dismissing the class, she tarried for a few minutes while packing her things, feeling happy at how well it had gone.

tassel

Noun | TASS – ul

A bunch of silk threads or threads of silklike material emerging from a point and dangling.

During the keynote speech, she reached up and adjusted the tassel on her graduation cap.

tawny

Adjective | TAW – nee

Tan colored, or yellowish brown.

Her friends barely recognized her because her hair had gotten tawny from all the Australian sun.

tea

Noun | TEE

The dried leaves of a shrub (*Camellia sinensis*) grown widely in China, Japan, and India, or an infusion of tea leaves in boiling water; any infusion of leaves in water in preparation of a beverage.

For her garden party, she set out a pitcher of fresh spearmint tea and her best cups.

telegram

Noun | TELL – uh – gram

A message sent by telegraph.

The telegram arrived at the hotel sometime overnight and was handed to him by the concierge at breakfast.

telegraph

Noun/Verb | TELL – uh – graf

An apparatus for transmitting messages over a distance, especially by means of electricity, in widespread use from the mid-19th century well into the 20th century; to convey or announce by telegraph or by other signals.

In the crowded office, Lincoln sat near the telegraph machines, nervous each time new results from the election came in.

tempo

Noun | TEM - poe

The measure of the rapidity of a rhythm, especially in music.

The drummer upped the tempo of the beat, which prompted the bassist to strum faster.

tendril

Noun | TEN - drul

A slender, often spiraling shoot of a plant by which it attaches itself to a support for climbing, or something tendril like.

It was incredible to watch the watermelon vines' tendrils wrap themselves around any solid object in their path.

terrace
Noun/Verb | TARE – us

Any raised, level place, of earth, as in farms adjacent to
bodies of water, or near structures; to make a terrace.

tent

Noun | TENT

An enclosable, portable shelter that consists of fabric—polyester usually—stretching over flexible poles.

Traditional bedouin tents are made from the woven hair of camels and black goats, and feature rooms separated by curtains.

terra-cotta

Noun | TARE – uh – COT – uh

A mixture of clay and sand, hardened by firing, orangish brown in color, and used especially for pots and statues.

The army of terra-cotta warrior statues had been buried for more than 2,000 years when it was discovered.

thermal

Adjective | THER – mul

Pertaining to heat.

Thermal vents in the ocean floor sustain life, even though it's very cold and completely dark all around them.

thorax

Noun | THOR – ax

The chest, or central part of a body, most commonly in reference to insects, having the legs and internal organs.

You can easily pick out the thorax of an ant—it's the middle one of its three body parts.

threshold

Noun | THRESH - hold

A piece of wood or stone under the door of a house, or the place or point of entering, literally or metaphorically.

The age of 15 is considered by some to mark the threshold between girlhood and womanhood, which is why the quinceañera celebration is such an important event for girls in parts of the United States and Latin America.

thrive

Verb | THRIVE

To prosper, do well, or flourish.

Surprisingly, the eggplants were thriving in the garden this year, which meant that the family was eating a lot of ratatouille.

tide

Noun | TIDE

The regular ebb and flow of the sea,
driven primarily by the gravity of the
moon as it orbits around the Earth.

thunder

Noun/Verb | THUN – der

The sharp cracking or steady rumbling sound in the atmosphere after a flash of lightning; to make thunder or sound like thunder.

He didn't believe her, that the forecast called for severe storms, until thunder shook the house.

tiger

Noun | TIE - ger

The biggest cat species (*Panthera tigris*), native to the eastern and southern portions of the Asian continent, easily identified by its stripes.

The tiger was known to live at a certain spot by the river.

timbre

Noun | TOM – bur

T tone, character, or quality of richness of a musical sound.

The electric guitar, connected to the two pedals, produced a sound with a complex timbre.

time
Noun/Verb | TIME

The process by which events happen in a linear sequence, one after the other; the measure of the flow of events; to measure a quantity of time.

Three months seemed like plenty of time to cast the rest of the movie, now that the lead actors had signed on.

tinge
Verb/Noun | TINJ

To tint or mix with something; a small amount of color or taste mixed into something else.

The boy swirled his cereal around, seeing how it tinged the milk with all its colors.

toadstool
Noun | TOAD – stool

A mushroom, generically, or the obtuse conical shape topping some mushrooms.

She was careful not to step on the new toadstools that had come up along the path in the woods.

together

Adverb | Too – GETH – er

Gathered in one place, or in the same place, time, or company.

Together, they had pop culture, sports, history, and science covered—they were ready to win trivia night.

tortoise

Noun | TOR – tuss

Reptiles of the family Testudinidae having a shell in two parts, the carapace above and the plastron below, to protect themselves from predators, often growing very large in size and old in age.

In Florida, gopher tortoises help over 350 other kinds of animals with the burrows they dig in the sandy soil.

trail

Noun/Verb | TRALE

A slight path, especially one that travels a significant distance; to track someone or something that has made such a path, or to carry or drag something behind oneself.

Because of the controlled burn, still smoldering, the rangers diverted the trail to the other side of the hill.

tranquility

Noun | Tran – KWILL – i – tee

The state of being quiet and peaceful.

In late spring every year, once the students have left, tranquility descends on the college campus.

transom

Noun | TRANS – um

A horizontal beam over a window or door, or a window above said beam.

In remodeling the old row house, they were pleasantly surprised to find historic transom windows hidden under the drywall.

travel

Verb/Noun | TRAV – ul

To go from one place to another, or to journey, or to move; the act of going from place to place.

"My thoughts are never clearer than when I'm traveling," she wrote in her journal.

treehouse

Noun | TREE – haus

A structure built up next to or around the trunk and major branches

trek

Noun/Verb | TREK

The distance from one place to another, usually large; to journey, typically by foot or other nonmotorized means.

The distance from his house to the corner market was usually no big deal, but in the blizzard, it became a daunting trek.

trellis

Noun/Verb | TREL – iss

A structure for supporting plants, often of crude or light, latticed woodwork; to build such a structure and prepare plants to climb it.

The cucumber trellis had fallen in the wind overnight, so in the morning they worked to put it back up.

triceratops

Noun | Try - SARE – i – tops

A ceratopsian dinosaur—with a parrot-like beak, bony frills, and often horns—of the late Cretaceous period, which ate palm fronds, grew to over 25 feet in length, and weighed up to over 12,000 pounds.

When thinking about which herbivorous dinosaurs would be best equipped to handle a T. rex attack, the triceratops, with its three nasty-looking horns and huge size, comes first to mind.

trickle

Verb/Noun | TRIK – ul

To flow gently or in a small stream; such a stream.

In the downpour, the gutter overflowed, and water trickled down the brick wall.

trowel

Noun/Verb | TROW - well

A tool used in spreading mortar, or, in gardening, to dig small holes or move small quantities of dirt; to use a trowel.

He troweled another scoop of sand into the pot to create looser soil.

trust

Noun/Verb | TRUST

Having faith in the integrity, conscientiousness, or truth of someone or something; to exercise this faith.

Being able to trust your friends is worth more than gold.

tuft
Noun/Verb | TUFT

A number of small things in a knot attached to something at the base end but not at the opposite end; a cluster, or a clump of grass or dirt; to create a tuft.

When the ball was kicked to the opposite end of the field, the goalkeeper took the opportunity to stamp down a tuft in the pitch at his feet.

tugboat
Noun | TUG – boat

A sturdy steamship for towing vessels, usually in harbors or ports.

The tugboat, pushing a huge container ship back out to sea, looked like it was the hardest-working boat in the harbor.

twig
Noun | TWIG

A small branch of a tree, often detached, leafless, and dry and used in the making of a fire.

He stepped on a twig, causing it to snap loudly, and the two small bears immediately turned and ran down the side of the ridge.

tulip

Noun | TEW – lip

A genus (*Tulipa*) of bulb-
growing plants having warm-
colored, bell-shaped flowers.

Uu

umbel

Noun | UM – bell

A form of flower in which a number of stalks, each bearing a flower, radiate from a center.

The umbels of elderflowers appeared in snowy white patches in the hedgerow.

undulating

Adverb | UN – dyoo – lay – ting

Moving like waves.

The art exhibition featured an entire room filled with sheets of undulating silk cloth.

unison

Noun | YOON – i – sen

All at once, or together, in the striking of a particular note, chord, or sound.

The band really got the crowd going when the guitarist and the keyboardist hit C major in unison.

universe

Noun | YOO – ne – vers

The entirety of all conceivable reality; the boundless container of all matter and space.

The universe is expanding, but some researchers believe that its expansion will eventually stop and then reverse itself, far in the future.

Utopia

Noun | Yoo - TOE – pee – uh

A perfectly ordered society in which all matters of society and government function for the benefit of all members of said society.

In Thomas More's book Utopia, *everybody eats together in communal dining halls and no one pays for their dinner.*

vast
Adjective | VAST

Of great extent or
expanse, or great in
amount or quantity.

vamp
Noun/Verb | VAMP

A woman who uses her charms to get what she wants; to act like a vamp, or to improvise in a wily way.

The pictures so far were boring looking, so she told the girls to vamp like they were in The Rocky Horror Picture Show.

vault
Noun/Verb | VAWLT

An arched roof or a chamber with an arched roof, especially one underground, or any room like such; to jump over something by means of a pole or by resting the hands on something.

They were famous for vaulting over the hood of their muscle car to save time.

vegetal
Adjective | VEH – jeh – tal

Of or relating to vegetation or plant growth.

Given the number of houseplants that had been brought inside for the winter, the dining room had a very vegetal feel all of a sudden.

vellum

Noun | VEL - um

Parchment prepared by lime baths and burnishing from the skins of certain animals, or slightly rough, tough paper.

"I know it's quicker to write with pen on paper," she said, "but there's something so satisfying about the feel of a calligraphy marker on vellum."

velvet

Noun/Adjective | VELV – it

A clothing and upholstery material known for its exceptional smoothness and softness; describing something as like velvet.

Whenever they visited her family in the South they had the best red velvet cake of their lives.

veneer

Verb/Noun | Veh – NEER

To cover one wood with a thin layer of another, more attractive wood, or to disguise with fake attractiveness; a thin coating or false appearance.

The veneer of walnut over the plywood made the den feel old-fashioned, stately even.

venetian

Adjective | Veh – NEE – shen

Of or belonging to Venice; describing window blinds formed of thin slips of wood, adjustable so as to allow in more or less light.

The Venetian Resort in Las Vegas, with its faux canals and faux outdoor dining patios, is a pretty good take on the actual Venice.

veranda

Noun | Veh – RAN – da

A covered balcony or open portico, with a roof sloping beyond the main building, supported by light pillars.

The party assembled on the veranda for tea before the big golf tournament.

verdigris

Noun | VER – de – grees

A greenish-blue deposit on copper, bronze, or brass that has been weathered over time.

The door knocker had, in the years since the family's departure, accumulated some verdigris that dampened its sound.

verge

Noun/Verb | VERJ

The extreme edge or horizon; in gardening or landscaping, the grass or wild growth edging of a cultivated or paved area; to border upon.

All along the verge of the field they planted the sycamore saplings.

vespers

Noun | VESS - per

In the church, the evening services; also, a certain gin-based cocktail.

The priest had no trouble picking out the opening hymn for the next evening's vespers.

village

Noun | VIL - uj

A small grouping of houses, less than a town.

The alpine village had a number of winter traditions that would seem alien to those from outside.

violet

Noun/Adjective | VYE – oh – let

A flowering plant belonging to the *Viola* genus, usually having hues of purple and blooming in early spring; the color of a violet: bluish purple.

Not much grows beneath the tall pine trees in that part of the woods, but you can count on the violets showing their flowers every April.

vitality

Noun | Vye – TAL – i – tee

The capacity to endure and flourish, or the strength of one's energy for living.

Studying the genealogical records, he wanted very much to know how his great-great-grandfather had had the vitality to live to the age of 105.

waffle

Noun/Verb | WAH – ful

A kind of batter cake with indented squares, once baked over an open fire in an iron utensil of hinged halves called a waffle iron but, now usually made in an electric waffle maker or toasted frozen; to waver indecisively.

As soon as the dining hall opened, there they were, trays at the ready, salivating for the famous Belgian waffles with syrup and strawberries.

wafting

Verb | WAHF - ting

Moving gently as a gas through air; to move around like something that is wafting.

The smell of French toast wafting from the griddle drew them from their bedrooms in the morning.

waistcoat

Noun | WEH – sket

A short coat worn just beneath the coat and fitting the waist tightly.

Every bartender at the speakeasy wore a waistcoat and knew how to make at least thirty cocktails.

walk
Verb/Noun | WALK

To convey oneself on foot with alternate steps, or to travel on foot;
the act or manner of walking, or that in or through which one walks,
or the distance walked over.

walkabout

Noun | WALK - uh - bout

A time of wandering, especially in connection to Australian Aborigine life, as a digression from quotidian life, or a journey similar to such.

"A walkabout," the speaker explained, "while uneasy to arrange in hectic modern life, can be a productive spiritual experience, as the Aborigines have known for thousands of years."

waltz

Noun/Verb | WAWLTZ

A German national dance performed by two people with a whirling motion, sometimes fast, or the music for such; to dance a waltz, or to walk with a certain panache.

The count, with his coattails flying, joined the waltz with as much energy as the rest of the party.

watercress

Noun | WAH – der – kress

A plant (*Nasturtium officinale*) in the Brassicacaea family that grows submerged in cool streams, whose leaves float and spread over the water, used in salads and, in the United Kingdom and Europe, as a green topping on sandwiches; sometimes shortened to "cress."

"Nothing beats an egg salad sandwich with cress when you're hungry on the move," his father would say.

waterfall

Noun | WAH – der – fawl

A straight-down descent of a body of water, such as a lake or river.

On one side of the roaring waterfall was Zambia; on the other, Zimbabwe.

waveform

Noun | WAYV – form

The representation of a wave, often sound, along x- and y-axes according to how its amplitude and frequency change over time, with sine, saw, square, and triangle being common examples.

If you set the synthesizer's LFO to the saw waveform, you'll get a buzzy sound, whereas if you set it to square, it'll sound thicker.

wedding

Noun | WED – ing

A ceremony of marriage, when two people are bonded to each other in love.

After two delayed dates, the wedding finally took place, in a rustic barn in Napa Valley.

wilderness

Noun | WIL - der - ness

A wild or uncultivated, untamed region.

weekend

Noun | WEE – kend

Saturday and Sunday, typically, and time off work and set aside for gatherings and diversion.

With the babysitter arranged and tickets to New York booked, the whole weekend would be a blissful return to the freedom of their younger days.

Wellingtons

Noun | WEL – ing – tunz

Boots, often waterproof, rising to or above the knee, or, formerly, a kind of high riding boots.

He was surprised at how well equipped the city's residents were to deal with January's high waters: everybody walked around in a pair of Wellingtons.

willow

Noun | WILL – oh

A tree or shrub of the genus *Salix*, having slender, easily bendable branches and graceful shapes, valued for its erosion control and shading qualities.

The willow tree hanging its branches over a pond in the yard is a common sight in Amish Country.

windlass
Noun/Verb | WIND – las

A simple machine consisting of a revolving cylinder and rope or chain used to haul up heavy objects, as a bucket from a well or a ship's anchor; to use a windlass.

The sailors worked together to turn the windlass so the ship could be on its way while the wind was good.

wings
Noun | WINGS

The appendages of a bird, or other animal or insect, or of an aircraft, by which it flies, or anything resembling wings.

She watched the blue heron beat its wings across the lake.

woven
Verb | WOVE – en

United together into cloth.

The sweater she'd received had been woven from pure Irish wool.

winter

Noun/Verb | WIN – ter

The cold season of the year, or any season
of cheerlessness; to spend the cold season
somewhere other than home, often warmer.

xanthic

Adjective | ZAN – thick

Yellow or yellowish.

He drew confused looks from his kids when he warned them, "Remember: don't eat the xanthic snow."

xenic

Adjective | ZEEN – ick

Containing unidentified organisms, especially bacteria; elusively foreign as in such a collection.

There was something xenic about the crowd of protesters, in the way that some of them dressed in loose-fitting tie-dyed shirts and stood quietly while others shouted.

xeric

Adjective | ZEER – ick

Dry, or describing something that only needs trace amounts of moisture.

In the chilly, high-altitude Gobi Desert, xeric plants such as the saxaul shrub, which stores what little moisture it gets in its spongy bark, show that life finds ways to thrive even in the harshest environments.

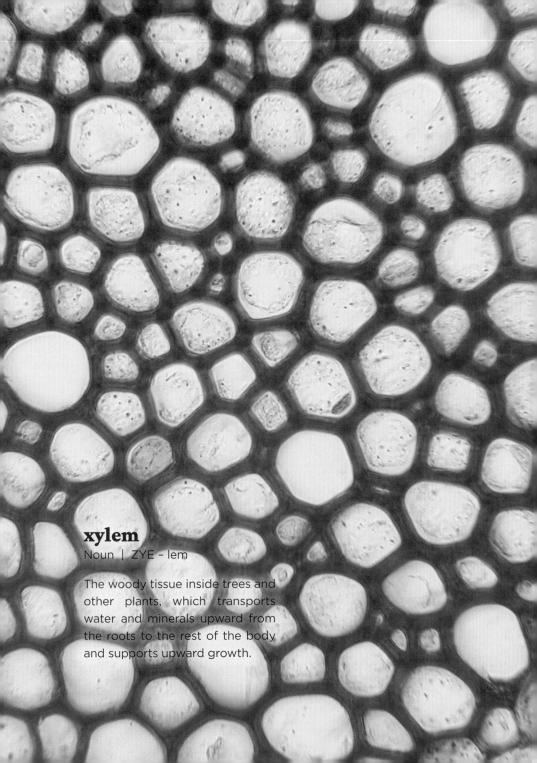

xylem

Noun | ZYE – lem

The woody tissue inside trees and other plants, which transports water and minerals upward from the roots to the rest of the body and supports upward growth.

yew
Noun | YOO

A tree of the genus *Taxus*, historically
planted in graveyards in Europe, and
whose wood has been used to make
bows, musical instruments, etc.

Yy

yonder

Adjective | YAWN – der

At some distance that is still within view.

"When the morning rises on yonder mountains," he said, "you'll notice how they look almost blue."

yodel

Verb | YO - dul

To sing in the style of the mountaineers of the Tyrolean Alps, quickly alternating the pitch of one's voice between normal notes and falsetto notes.

She practiced yodeling on her way up the steep mountainside, listening for the echoes of her voice.

Yule log

Noun | YOOL – log

The block of wood cut down in the forest or preserved from last winter season's holidays, brought back to the house and set on fire in celebration of Christmas.

Every year, even if it's cold and snowy, we burn a Yule log in the backyard firepit to kick off Christmas.

Zz

zeitgeist
Noun | ZITE - guyst

The spirit of the age, or the prevailing feeling of the times.

She said, "I'd love to time travel to Greenwich Village in the 1950s, just to pick up on the zeitgeist."

zest
Noun | ZEST

Something that adds sharp flavor, as the gratings from a lemon or lime peel; enjoyment or relish.

His zest for sailing meant that he was away from the office quite a bit.

zygote
Noun | ZIGH – goat

The beginning of new life (other than bacteria), as represented by a fertilized egg, or the combination of two individual strains of DNA.

We're all individuals, with our own ways of life and preferences, but at the end of the day, we were all zygotes once.

zephyr

Noun | ZEH – fir

A gentle breeze or western wind.

lighthouse

see page 120

toadstool
see page 206

About Cider Mill Press Book Publishers

Good ideas ripen with time. From seed to harvest, Cider Mill Press brings
fine reading, information, and entertainment together between the covers
of its creatively crafted books. Our Cider Mill bears fruit twice a year,
publishing a new crop of titles each spring and fall.

"Where Good Books Are Ready for Press"

501 Nelson Place
Nashville, TN 37214

cidermillpress.com